CRC Series on
COMPUTER-AIDED ENGINEERING

Series Editor: *Hojjat Adeli*

Neurocomputing for Design Automation
Hojjat Adeli and Hyo Seon Park

High Performance Computing in Structural Engineering
Hojjat Adeli and Roesdiman Soegiarso

Distributed Computer-Aided Engineering
Hojjat Adeli and Sanjay Kumar

NEUROCOMPUTING
for DESIGN
AUTOMATION

Hojjat Adeli
The Ohio State University, U.S.A.

Hyo Seon Park
Yeungnam University, Korea

CRC Press
Boca Raton Boston London New York Washington, D.C.

Library of Congress Cataloging-in-Publication Data

Adeli, Hojjat, 1950–
    Neurocomputing for design automation / Hojjat Adeli, Hyo Seon
Park.
        p.   cm. -- (Computer-aided engineering)
    Includes bibliographical references and index.
    ISBN 0-8493-2092-5 (alk. paper)
    1. Structural design--Data processing. 2. Computer-aided design.
3. Neural computers. I. Park, Hyo Seon. II. Title. III. Series:
Computer-aided engineering (Boca Raton, Fla.)
TA658.2A34 1998
624.1'771'0285—dc21   98-12674
                                                                                                                    CIP

No claim to original U.S. Government works
International Standard Book Number 0-8493-2092-5
Library of Congress Card Number 98-12674
Printed in the United States of America 1 2 3 4 5 6 7 8 9 0
Printed on acid-free paper

Preface

This book presents a summary of our research in the area of design automation performed during the past few years. A patent application was submitted for this innovative work to the *U.S. Patent and Trademark Office* in April 1996. The patent was approved under *"Efficient Design Automation and Optimization, and Structures Produced Thereby"* in August 1997.

Automation of design of large one-of-a-kind engineering systems is considered a particularly challenging problem. The computational models and algorithms presented in this book have been applied to large one-of-a-kind structural design problems. But, they can also be applied to other types of large-scale engineering design such as aerospace design, mechanical design, and electronic design, because they all have the same common fundamental characteristics: a) they are open-ended and the optimum solution must be chosen among a very large number of potential solutions and b) their design is based on complex highly nonlinear and implicit design constraints. The computational model and algorithms presented in the book yield consistently robust results no matter how large the size of the problems, how irregular the structure, or how complicated the constraints. This work demonstrates how a new level is achieved in design automation of one-of-a-kind engineering systems through

the ingenious use and integration of a novel computational paradigm, mathematical optimization, and new high-performance computer architecture.

Hojjat Adeli and Hyo Seon Park

September 1997

About the authors

Hojjat Adeli received his Ph.D. from Stanford University in
1976. He is currently Professor of Civil and Environmental Engineering and Geodetic Science, Founder and Director of Knowledge Engineering Lab, and a member of the Center for Cognitive Science at The Ohio State University. A contributor to 46
different research journals, he has authored over 300 research
and scientific publications in diverse engineering and computer
science disciplines. Professor Adeli has authored/co-authored
five pioneering books including *Parallel Processing in Structural Engineering*, Elsevier, 1993, and *Machine Learning-Neural
Networks, Genetic Algorithms, and Fuzzy Systems*, John Wiley, 1995. He has also edited 12 books including *Knowledge
Engineering - Volume One Fundamentals, Knowledge Engineering - Volume Two Applications*, McGraw-Hill, 1990; *Parallel
Processing in Computational Mechanics*, Marcel Dekker, 1992;
Supercomputing in Engineering Analysis, Marcel Dekker, 1992;
and *Advances in Design Optimization*, Chapman and Hall, 1994.
Professor Adeli is the Founder and Editor-in-Chief of the research journals *Computer-Aided Civil and Infrastructure Engineering* which he founded in 1986 and *Integrated Computer-Aided Engineering* which he founded in 1993. He is the recipient of numerous academic, research, and leadership awards,

honors, and recognition. He is listed in 24 Who's Whos and archival biographical listings such as *Two Thousands Notable Americans* and *Five Hundred Leaders of Influence*. He has been an organizer or contributor to 103 conferences held in 34 different countries. He was a Keynote/Plenary Lecturer at international computing conferences held in Italy (1989), Mexico (1991), Japan (1991), China (1992), Canada (1992, 1996), Portugal (1992), U.S. (1993, 1995, 1996), Germany (1993), Morocco (1994), Singapore (1994, 1996), Australia (1995), Bulgaria (1997), Lithuania (1996), Iran (1997), France (1997), and the Bahamas (1997). Professor Adeli's research has been recognized and sponsored by government funding agencies such as the *National Science Foundation, Federal Highway Administration*, and *U.S. Air Force's Flight Dynamics Lab*, professional organizations such as the *American Iron and Steel Institute* (AISI), the *American Institute of Steel Construction* (AISC), state agencies such as the *Ohio Department of Transportation* and *Ohio Department of Development*, and private industry such as Cray Research Inc. and Bethlehem Steel Corporation. He is a Fellow of the *World Literary Academy* and *American Society of Civil Engineers*.

H.S. Park received his Ph.D. from The Ohio State University in 1995. He was a senior researcher and software developer at *Daewoo Institute of Construction Technology*, one of the largest and leading research and development firms in Korea. He is currently an Assistant Professor at *Yeungnam University* in Korea. Dr. Park is the co-author of seven research articles in the area of neural network computing.

Acknowledgment

The work presented in this book was partially sponsored by the *National Science Foundation, American Iron and Steel Institute*, and *American Institute of Steel Construction* under grants to the senior author. Supercomputing time on the Cray YMP machine was provided by the *Ohio Supercomputer Center* and on the CM-5 was provided by *National Center for Supercomputing Applications* at the University of Illinois at Urbana-Champaign. Parts of the research presented in this book were published in several journal articles in *Computers and Structures* (published by Pergamon Press), *Microcomputers in Civil Engineering* (published by Blackwell Publishers), *Journal of Structural Engineering* (published by American Society of Civil Engineers), *Neural Networks* (published by Pergamon Press), and the *AI Magazine* (published by the American Association for Artificial Intelligence), as noted in the list of references.

dedicated to

Nahid, Anahita, Amir Kevin, Mona, and Cyrus Adeli

and

Kang Jun, Chung Hyeok, and Su Mi Park

Contents

Chapter 1

Introduction

Automation of design of one-of-a-kind engineering systems is considered a particularly challenging problem. The senior author and his associates have been working on creating novel design theories and computational models with two broad objectives: automation and optimization (Abuyounes and Adeli, 1987; Adeli and Alrijieh, 1987; Adeli and Balasubramanyam, 1988; Paek and Adeli, 1988a & b; Adeli and Mark, 1988 & 1990; Adeli and Chompooming, 1989; Adeli and Ge, 1989; Adeli and Yeh, 1989; Eisenloffel and Adeli, 1990 & 1993; Yu and Adeli, 1991; Adeli and Hawkins, 1991; Adeli and Kamal, 1993; Adeli and Yu, 1993a & b, Adeli and Cheng, 1993 & 1994a; Adeli and Hung, 1995; Adeli and Kumar, 1995a; Kumar and Adeli, 1995a & b; Adeli and Sarma, 1995; Adeli and Kao, 1996; Kao and Adeli, 1997; Soegiarso and Adeli, 1996 & 1997a & b).

Civil engineering structures are usually one of a kind as opposed to manufacturing designs that are often mass produced. To create computational models for structural design automation we have been exploring new computing paradigms. Two such paradigms are neurocomputing and parallel processing. We will show how computationally elegant algorithms based on integration of a novel connectionist computing model, mathematical optimization, and massively parallel computer architecture can be used to automate the complex process of engineering design.

In Chapter 2 we explore the use of counterpropagation networks in structural engineering. The performance of counterpropagation is compared with that of the backpropagation algorithm. In Chapter 3 we present a neural dynamics model for optimal design of structures by the integrating penalty function method, Lyapunov stability theorem, Kuhn-Tucker conditions, and the neural dynamics concept. Neural dynamics is defined by a system of first-order differential equations governing time evolution changes in node (neuron) activations. A pseudo-objective function in the form of a Lyapunov energy functional is defined using the exterior penalty function method. The Lyapunov stability theorem guarantees that solutions of the corresponding dynamic system (trajectories) for arbitrarily given starting points approach an equilibrium point without increasing the value of the objective function. In other words, the new neural dynamics model for structural optimization problems guarantees global convergence and robustness; but, this does not guarantee the equilibrium point is a local minimum. We use the Kuhn-Tucker conditions to verify that an equilibrium point satisfies the necessary conditions for a local minimum. In other word, a learning rule is developed by integrating the Kuhn-Tucker necessary conditions for a local minimum with the formulated Lyapunov function.

In Chapter 4 the neural dynamics model is applied to a linear optimization problem, the minimum weight plastic design of low-rise planar steel frames. In this application, nonlinear code-specified constraints are not used. It is shown that the neural dynamics model yields stable results no matter how the starting point is selected.

In Chapter 5 we develop a nonlinear neural dynamics model

for optimization of large space structures. The model consists of two information flow control components and two information server components. The first component is a neural dynamics system of differential equations, which corresponds to a learning rule governing time evolutionary changes in nodes activations. The second component is the network topology with one variable layer and as many constraint layers as the number of loading conditions. The first information server component performs finite element analysis and finds the magnitudes of constraint violations. The other information server finds the design sensitivity coefficients. The nonlinear neural dynamics model is applied to the minimum weight design of four example structures. It is concluded that the new approach results in a highly robust algorithm for optimization of large structures.

In order to achieve automated optimum design of realistic structures subjected to actual design constraints of commonly used design codes such as the American Institute of Steel Construction (AISC) Allowable Stress Design (ASD) and Load and Resistance Factor Design (LRFD) specifications (AISC, 1989 & 1994), in Chapter 6 we present a hybrid counterpropagation neural (CPN) network-neural dynamics model for discrete optimization of structures consisting of commercially available sections such as the wide-flange (W) shapes used in steel structures.

Optimization of large structures with thousands of members subjected to actual constraints of commonly used codes requires an inordinate amount of computer processing time and can be done on multiprocessor supercomputers (Adeli, 1992a & b). A high degree of parallelism can be exploited in neural computing models (Adeli and Hung, 1995). Consequently, in Chapter 7 we present a data parallel neural dynamics model for discrete optimization of large steel structures and describe its implementation on the massively parallel Connection Machine CM-5 system.

In the final chapter we present distributed nonlinear neural dynamics algorithms for discrete optimization of large structures and describe their implementation on a distributed memory machine, the CRAY T3D. A worksharing preconditioned conjugate gradient algorithm is presented for the solution of the resulting linear equations.

The neural dynamics algorithms developed in this work have been applied to structures of arbitrary size and configuration, including very large superhigh-rise building structures with more than 20,000 members that are subjected to the constraints of the AISC's ASD and LRFD specifications and multiple loading conditions including wind loading according to the UBC code (UBC, 1994).

An attractive characteristic of our neural dynamics model is its robustness and stability. We find that the model is insensitive to the selection of the initial design. This is especially noteworthy because we apply the model to optimization of large space frame structures subjected to actual design constraints of the AISC's ASD and LRFD codes. In particular, the constraints of the LRFD code are complicated and highly nonlinear implicit functions of design variables. This work demonstrates how a new level is achieved in design automation of one-of-a-kind engineering systems through the ingenious use and integration of a novel computational paradigm, mathematical optimization, and new high-performance computer architecture.

Chapter 2

Counterpropagation Neural Networks in Structural Engineering

2.1 Introduction

In the first structural engineering application of neural networks published in an archival journal, Adeli and Yeh (1989) presented a model of machine learning in engineering design based on the concept of self-adjustment of internal control parameters and perceptron. The problem of structural design was cast in a form to be described by a perceptron without hidden layers.

Vanluchene and Sun (1990) discuss the use of the backpropagation learning algorithm (Rumelhart et al., 1986) in structural engineering. Hung and Adeli (1991a) present a two-layer neural network learning model for engineering design by combining the perceptron with a single-layer AND neural net. They reported improvement in the rate of learning compared with the single-layer perceptron learning model. Several other researchers have applied neural networks, mostly backpropagation algorithms, in structural engineering and mechanics and related engineering problems (Hajela and Berke, 1991; Ghaboussi et al., 1991; Masri et al., 1993; Kang and Yoon, 1994; Messner et al., 1994;

Stephens and Vanluchene, 1994; Elkordy et al., 1994; and Hurson et al., 1994).

Hung and Adeli (1994a) present a multilayer neural network development environment for effective implementation of learning algorithms for the domain of engineering design using the object-oriented programming paradigm (Adeli and Yu, 1993a & b; Yu and Adeli, 1993). It consists of five primary components: learning domain, neural nets, library of learning strategies, learning process, and analysis process. These components have been implemented as five classes in the object-oriented programming language C++. The library of learning strategies includes generalized delta rule with error backpropagation.

Adeli and Zhang (1993) present an improved perceptron learning algorithm by introducing an adjustment factor in each self-modification iteration of the original perceptron learning model. The adjustment factor in each iteration is determined such that the domain error is reduced in the subsequent iterations. The application of the new algorithm to structural design problems demonstrates its superior convergence property.

Gunaratnam and Gero (1994) discuss the effect of representation on the performance of neural networks in structural engineering applications using the error backpropagation algorithm. They suggest that dimensional analysis provides a suitable representation framework for training the input/output pattern pairs.

Backpropagation seems to be the most utilized neural network algorithm in civil engineering disciplines. This is primarily due to its simplicity. A detailed discussion of the backpropagation algorithm with a view on engineering applications can be found in Hegazy et al. (1994). They also provide a structured framework for developing practical neural network applications.

The backpropagation algorithm, however, has a slow rate of learning. Consequently, it can not be readily applied to large problems. One approach to improving the learning performance is the development of parallel algorithms on multiprocessor machines (Adeli, 1992a & b). Hung and Adeli (1993) present parallel backpropagation learning algorithms employing the microtasking and vectorization capabilities of vector MIMD machines such as the Cray YMP8/864 supercomputer (Saleh and Adeli, 1994a).

How to improve the convergence speed of neural networks' learning algorithms is of significant importance and is currently being actively researched (Hung and Adeli, 1991b; Adeli and Hung, 1993a & b; Hung and Adeli, 1994b). Adeli and Hung (1994) present an adaptive conjugate learning algorithm for training multilayer feedforward neural networks. The problem of arbitrary trial-and-error selection of the learning and momentum ratios encountered in the momentum backpropagation algorithm is circumvented in the new adaptive algorithm. Instead of constant learning and momentum ratios, the step length in the inexact line search is adapted during the learning process through a mathematical approach. Thus, the new adaptive algorithm provides a more solid mathematical foundation for neural network learning. The algorithm has been applied to two different domains: engineering design and image recognition. It is shown that the adaptive neural networks algorithm has a superior convergence property compared with the momentum backpropagation algorithm.

In this chapter, we explore the use of counterpropagation networks in structural engineering. In contrast to backpropagation which is a supervised learning algorithm, a counterpropagation network is a combination of supervised and unsupervised (self-organizing) mapping neural networks (Hecht-Neilsen, 1987a & b). The performances of backpropagation and counterpropagation learning algorithms are compared for structural engineering applications. Four examples are presented. The first two examples are taken from the literature for the sake of comparison. They are the concrete beam design and the prediction of the maximum bending moment in a simply supported plate (Vanluchene and Sun, 1990; Gunaratnam and Gero, 1994). The other two examples are new. The first one is the prediction of the critical elastic lateral torsional buckling moment of beams. The second one is the prediction of the moment-gradient coefficient C_b for doubly and singly symmetric steel beams.

2.2   Counterpropagation

The backpropagation algorithm has been covered extensively in recent literature (Rumelhart et al., 1986; Hung and Adeli, 1993) and, therefore, will not be described here. We will, however, review the counterpropagation algorithm briefly in this section (Woods, 1988). The topology of a counterpropagation network consists of three primary layers: input layer, competition layer, and interpolation layer (Figure 2.1).

For training the network, the vectors of input training instances $\mathbf{X}$ and desired output $\mathbf{Y}$ are presented to the network at the input and interpolation layer, respectively. Thus, the number of nodes in the input and interpolation layers correspond to the number of elements in the vectors $\mathbf{X}$ and $\mathbf{Y}$, respectively. The vector of computed output is represented by

INPUT (**X**)   COMPETITION   INTERPOLATION   INPUT (**X**)   OUTPUT (**Y'**)
          LAYER   LAYER

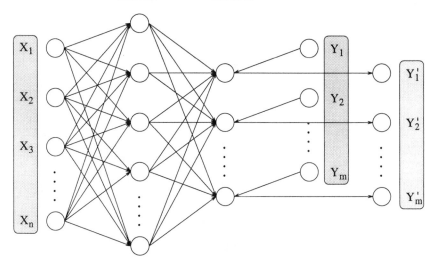

FIGURE 2.1 Topology of a counterpropagation network

$\mathbf{Y'}$. A counterpropagation network is trained in two successive steps. The counterpropagation learning algorithm is presented schematically in Figure 2.2.

     The first step is performed between the input layer and the competition layer. For each pair of training instance and desired output $(\mathbf{X}, \mathbf{Y})$, each component of the training instance, X_i, is presented to the corresponding node of the input layer. Let $\mathbf{U}_j$ be the arbitrary initial weight vector assigned to the links between the input nodes and the jth node in the competition layer. The transfer function for the competition layer is defined

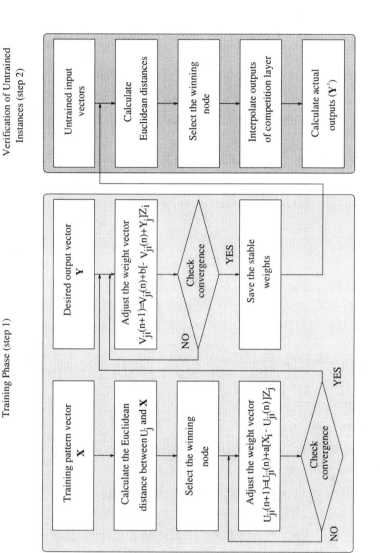

FIGURE 2.2 Counterpropagation learning algorithm

by the Euclidean distance between the weight vector $\mathbf{U}_j$ and the training instance $\mathbf{X}$ as follows:

$$d_j = \| \mathbf{U}_j - \mathbf{X} \| \tag{2.1}$$

where $\| \mathbf{X} \| = \sqrt{\sum_j |X_j|^2}$. For the given training instance $\mathbf{X}$, each node in the competition layer competes with other nodes and the node with the shortest Euclidean distance to $\mathbf{X}$ wins. As a result of the competition, the output of the winning node is set to 1.0 and outputs of the other nodes are set to 0. Thus the output of the jth node in the competition layer, Z_j, is given by

$$Z_j = \begin{cases} 1.0 & : \quad if \quad d_j < d_i \quad for \quad all \quad i \\ 0 & : \quad otherwise \end{cases} \tag{2.2}$$

A weight, U_{ji}, assigned to the link connecting the node j in the competition layer and the node i in the input layer is adjusted according to the Kohonen (1988) learning rule:

$$U_{ji}(n+1) = U_{ji}(n) + a[X_i - U_{ji}(n)]Z_j \tag{2.3}$$

where n is the iteration number and a is the learning coefficient. For the learning coefficient, Hecht-Neilsen (1988) suggests a number in the range of $0 < a \leq 0.8$. In this work, however, we define the learning coefficient, a, as a function of iteration number in the following form

$$a = \frac{1}{(n+1)^2} \tag{2.4}$$

After the weight vector, $\mathbf{U}_j$, of the competition layer stabilizes, the interpolation layer starts to learn the desired output.

The weight assigned to the link between the winning node i
in the competition layer and the jth node in the interpolation
layer, V_{ji}, is adjusted according to the learning rule suggested
by Grossberg (1982):

$$V_{ji}(n+1) = V_{ji}(n) + b[V_{ji}(n) + Y_j]Z_i \qquad (2.5)$$

where b is the learning coefficient. Hecht-Neilsen (1988) suggests
a number in the range of $0 < a \leq 1.0$. But, again in this work we
use Eq. (2.4) which we find more reasonable. The interpolation
layer uses a weighted summation function as a transfer function.
The jth element of the computed output of the network, Y_j', is
determined by

$$Y_j' = \sum_i V_{ji}Z_i \qquad (2.6)$$

During training (step 1 in Figure 2.2) only one node of
the competition layer can win and the corresponding output is
set to 1.0. After connection weights in a network stabilize, the
performance of the network can be tested by using untrained
instances. During the verification of untrained instances (step 2
in Figure 2.2) the number of winning nodes in the competition
layer can be more than one. The nonzero outputs of winning
nodes are set such that the node associated with the weight
vector closest to the given untrained instance has the largest
output. However, the sum of the outputs of winning nodes in
the competition layer remains equal to 1.0. By letting n_{win} be
the number of winning nodes in the competition layer and S_W
be the set of winning nodes, we define Z_j as follows:

$$
Z_j = \begin{cases} \dfrac{\left(\displaystyle\sum_{n=1}^{n_{win}} d_k\right) - d_j}{2\displaystyle\sum_{k=1}^{n_{win}} d_k} & if \;\; Z_j \in S_W \\[2em] 0 & if \;\; Z_j \notin S_W \end{cases} \tag{2.7}
$$

where d_k is the Euclidean distance between the weight vector assigned to the kth winning node and the untrained instance. Thus, the output of the network for untrained instances is calculated by Eq. (2.6) with more than one nonzero output from the competition layer, Z_j.

The selection of the number of the winning nodes is problem dependent and plays an important role in the performance of a counterpropagation network. Different numbers of winning nodes in the competition layer (different numbers of nonzero outputs from the competition layer) show different performance.

2.3 Comparison of Backpropagation with Counterpropagation

In order to compare the performances of backpropagation and counterpropagation neural network algorithms, two examples solved by Vanluchene and Sun (1990) are considered. A three-layer backpropagation network was used in these examples. Subsequently, Gunaratnam and Gero (1994) reported improved performance for these examples by using dimensionless parameters. Hence, we use the dimensionless parameters in both examples for comparisons of learning results and CPU time.

2.3.1   Concrete beam design example

This example is to find a mapping neural network that defines the relationship between M_u (ultimate bending moment) and d (depth of a reinforced concrete beam with a rectangular cross-section). The relationship requires six variables: ρ (reinforcement ratio), f_y (yield stress of reinforcing steel), f'_c (compressive strength of concrete), b (width of the rectangular beam), M_u, and d. This problem can be expressed in terms of two nondimensional variables $\rho f_y / f'_c$ and $M_u / f'_c bd^2$ as follows :

$$\rho \frac{f_y}{f'_c} = \varphi \left(\frac{M_u}{f'_c bd^2} \right) \tag{2.8}$$

where φ is the function defining the relationship. The objective of neural networks is to find the relationship function φ. We first used the same network topology of Gunaratnam and Gero (1994): one input node, one output node, and a hidden layer with three nodes, identified as BPN (1-3-1) in Table 2.1. Twenty-one training instances and ten untrained instances given in Table 2.1 were used for training and verification of the network. In order to reduce the error, we also used a network with one input node, one output node, and one hidden layer having eight nodes, identified as BPN (1-8-1) in Table 2.1. Training a backpropagation network with instantaneous updating took 23.50 and 26.65 CPU seconds on the Cray YMP8/864, for the two aforementioned networks, respectively. The percentage errors for the verification instances were reduced when the three hidden nodes were replaced with eight hidden nodes.

The topology of the counterpropagation network used in this work consists of one input node, twenty-one competition nodes, and one interpolation node, identified as CPN (1-21-1) in Table 2.1. It took only 0.008 CPU seconds for both training

Table 2.1 Learning results for the concrete beam design problem

Untrained instance number	$\dfrac{M_u}{f'_c bd^2}$	$\rho\dfrac{f_y}{f_c}$	G & G (1994) BPN (1-3-1)		BPN (1-8-1)		CPN (1-21-1)	
			Computed Output	Error (%)	Computed Output	Error (%)	Computed Output	Error (%)
1	0.1761	0.2267	0.2272	0.22	0.2259	0.35	0.2239	1.25
2	0.1673	0.2133	0.2147	0.65	0.2128	0.23	0.2444	0.53
3	0.1596	0.2000	0.2037	1.82	0.2013	0.65	0.2002	0.09
4	0.1894	0.2400	0.2460	2.44	0.2452	2.12	0.2448	1.97
5	0.1660	0.2100	0.2129	1.36	0.2109	0.43	0.2080	0.97
6	0.1770	0.2280	0.2285	0.22	0.2273	0.31	0.2250	1.33
7	0.0922	0.1100	0.1056	4.17	0.1076	2.23	0.1114	1.26
8	0.1332	0.1650	0.1656	0.36	0.1619	1.91	0.1596	3.38
9	0.0910	0.1080	0.1039	3.95	0.1062	1.69	0.1098	1.68
10	0.1445	0.1800	0.1820	1.10	0.1786	0.78	0.1732	3.93
CPU time on Cray YMP8/864			23.50 sec		26.65 sec		0.008 sec	

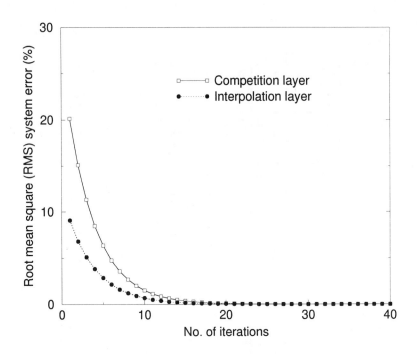

FIGURE 2.3 Convergence behavior of counterpropagation

of the same twenty-one instances and testing the ten untrained instances on the Cray YMP8/864. Thus, for this example the counterpropagation algorithm is nearly 3000 times more efficient than the backpropagation algorithm, where two networks produce comparable errors in testing of untrained instances. Figure 2.3 shows the convergence behavior for both competition and interpolation layers.

We observe that the proposed equation for estimating the learning coefficients a and b (Eq. 2.4) provides rapid convergence. Furthermore, the problem of arbitrary trial-and-error selection of learning and momentum ratios encountered in the backpropagation learning algorithm is circumvented since the coefficients a and b are computed automatically in each iteration without any user input.

2.3.2 Simply supported plate example

As an application of neural networks to structural analysis problems, this example is the prediction of the locations and magnitudes of maximum moments in a simply supported rectangular plate subjected to a unit concentrated load somewhere on the plate. In this example, each instance consists of four components: the dimensions of the plate in the X and Y directions and the locations of the load in the corresponding coordinates. The desired output vector has six components: the maximum bending moments M_x and M_y and the X and Y coordinates of their locations. The backpropagation results in Table 2.2 are from Gunaratnam and Gero (1994) for a network with four input nodes, two six-node hidden layers, and six output nodes. Thirty training instances and twelve untrained instances from finite element analysis were used for training and verification of the network, respectively.

In our counterpropagation network, we used four input nodes, one competition layer with thirty nodes, and six interpolation (output) nodes and the same training and verification instances. During the verification step, according to Eq. (2.7) two winning nodes in the competition layer with the best performance were selected for calculating the output of untrained instances. The learning results are compared with the results from the backpropagation network in Table 2.2. Figure 2.4 indicates clearly that the maximum percentage error of bending

Table 2.2   Learning results for the simply supported plate

Input				Desired output			Bending about X axis						
Plate dimension		Load position					Computed output						
							G & G (1994) BPN (4-6-6-4)			CPN (4-30-6)			
X	Y	X	Y	M_x	X	Y	M_x	X	Y	M_x	X	Y	
1.00	1.00	0.75	0.50	0.30	0.73	0.50	0.32	0.74	0.52	0.31	0.63	0.44	
1.00	1.00	0.90	0.80	0.21	0.88	0.77	0.17	0.91	0.83	0.20	0.78	0.76	
0.90	1.00	0.18	0.20	0.25	0.20	0.22	0.26	0.18	0.22	0.25	0.20	0.22	
0.90	1.00	0.22	0.80	0.26	0.25	0.73	0.27	0.24	0.77	0.27	0.21	0.74	
1.00	0.80	0.60	0.12	0.22	0.57	0.14	0.22	0.58	0.14	0.22	0.57	0.14	
1.00	0.80	0.80	0.20	0.26	0.77	0.22	0.25	0.76	0.22	0.25	0.77	0.23	
0.70	1.00	0.35	0.50	0.33	0.35	0.50	0.32	0.35	0.49	0.32	0.33	0.50	
0.70	1.00	0.56	0.90	0.21	0.54	0.88	0.25	0.46	0.74	0.22	0.46	0.62	
0.60	1.00	0.30	0.75	0.30	0.30	0.73	0.30	0.30	0.74	0.29	0.30	0.74	
1.00	0.60	0.90	0.48	0.20	0.88	0.47	0.25	0.85	0.41	0.25	0.81	0.51	
0.50	1.00	0.10	0.20	0.25	0.11	0.22	0.25	0.07	0.23	0.26	0.19	0.22	
0.50	0.50	0.20	0.38	0.23	0.22	0.36	0.24	0.18	0.32	0.24	0.34	0.19	

Input				Desired output			Bending about Y axis					
Plate dimension		Load position					Computed output					
							G & G (1994) BPN (4-6-4)			CPN (4-30-6)		
X	Y	X	Y	M_y	X	Y	M_y	X	Y	M_y	X	Y
1.00	1.00	0.75	0.50	0.29	0.73	0.50	0.30	0.74	0.52	0.31	0.63	0.44
1.00	1.00	0.90	0.80	0.19	0.88	0.77	0.12	0.91	0.83	0.21	0.78	0.76
0.90	1.00	0.18	0.20	0.25	0.20	0.22	0.25	0.18	0.22	0.25	0.20	0.22
0.90	1.00	0.18	0.20	0.26	0.25	0.73	0.26	0.24	0.77	0.26	0.21	0.74
1.00	0.80	0.60	0.12	0.26	0.57	0.14	0.26	0.58	0.14	0.26	0.57	0.14
1.00	0.80	0.80	0.20	0.27	0.77	0.22	0.27	0.76	0.22	0.27	0.77	0.23
0.70	1.00	0.35	0.50	0.30	0.35	0.50	0.30	0.35	0.50	0.29	0.33	0.50
0.70	1.00	0.56	0.90	0.21	0.54	0.88	0.27	0.46	0.74	0.23	0.46	0.62
0.60	1.00	0.30	0.75	0.28	0.30	0.73	0.28	0.32	0.74	0.28	0.30	0.74
1.00	0.60	0.90	0.48	0.21	0.88	0.47	0.26	0.85	0.41	0.25	0.81	0.51
0.50	1.00	0.10	0.20	0.21	0.11	0.22	0.22	0.07	0.23	0.23	0.19	0.22
0.50	0.50	0.20	0.38	0.26	0.22	0.36	0.27	0.18	0.32	0.28	0.34	0.19

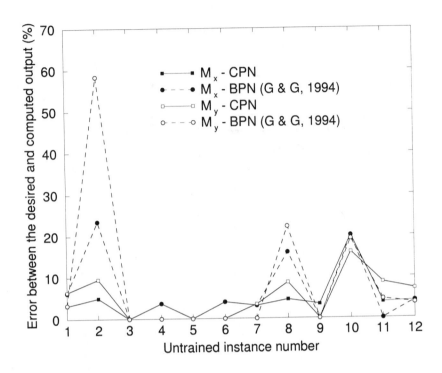

FIGURE 2.4 Comparison of learning results for BPN and CPN

moments in both directions for untrained instances is much lower for the counterpropagation network.

Training the counterpropagation network took 0.029 CPU seconds on the Cray YMP8/864 and approximately 3 seconds on a 486-based microcomputer. According to Vanluchene and Sun (1990), training the backpropagation network required approximately 32 hours of CPU time on a personal computer (the type of processor was not specified).

2.4 Application to Large Networks

The two examples presented in the previous sections used small networks. In this section, we apply the counterpropagation neural network to two structural engineering problems that require large networks.

2.4.1 Lateral torsional buckling of steel beams

This example is the prediction of elastic critical lateral torsional buckling moments of wide-flange steel beams (W shapes) subjected to a uniform bending moment (Figure 2.5). Two different boundary conditions are considered: a) simple supports where beam ends are restrained against twisting and lateral translation, but free to rotate and warp; and b) fixed supports where beam ends are restrained against lateral displacement and warping, but are free to rotate about the horizontal axis.

Twenty-eight different W shapes from the American Institute of Steel Construction (AISC) Allowable Stress Design (ASD) specifications (AISC, 1989) are used as training instances (Table 2.3).

The input for training and verification instances are the W shape designations (the nominal depth and weight per unit length), and the length of the beam. The beam length is increased from 6 m to 12 m in increments of 1.0 m. Thus, seven different lengths are used for each given W shape and the total number of training instances is 196.

For testing the network, ten different W shapes from the AISC's ASD specifications (AISC, 1989) are used (Table 2.3). For each untrained instance, the beam length is changed from

Table 2.3   Training and verification instances for LTB of steel beams

Training data for lateral torsional buckling of steel beams

Training instance	Designation	Training instance	Designation	Training instance	Designation
1	W 36 x 300	11	W 33 x 141	21	W27 x 114
2	W 36 x 260	12	W 33 x 118	22	W27 x 102
3	W 36 x 230	13	W 30 x 211	23	W27 x 84
4	W 36 x 194	14	W 30 x 173	24	W24 x 131
5	W 36 x 170	15	W 30 x 132	25	W24 x 104
6	W 36 x 150	16	W 30 x 124	26	W24 x 84
7	W 36 x 135	17	W 30 x 108	27	W24 x 69
8	W 33 x 241	18	W 30 x 90	28	W24 x 55
9	W 33 x 201	19	W 27 x 178		
10	W 33 x 152	20	W 27 x 146		

Verification data for lateral torsional buckling of steel beams

Verification instance	Designation	Verification instance	Designation	Verification instance	Designation
1	W 36 x 280	5	W 30 x 191	9	W24 x 117
2	W 36 x 160	6	W 30 x 116	10	W24 x 76
3	W 33 x 221	7	W 27 x 161		
4	W 33 x 134	8	W 27 x 94		

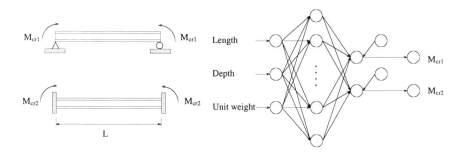

FIGURE 2.5 Counterpropagation for the lateral torsional buckling problem

6.5 m to 11.5 m in increments of 1.0 m. Thus, the trained network was tested using sixty untrained instances. The desired outputs consist of two elastic critical lateral torsional moments corresponding to the simply supported beam (M_{cr1}) and fixed-end beam (M_{cr2}) for the given length (L). They are computed from the closed form solutions (Chen and Lui, 1987):

$$M_{cr1} = \frac{\pi}{L}\sqrt{EI_yGJ\left[1 + \frac{\pi^2 EC_w}{GJL^2}\right]} \tag{2.9}$$

$$M_{cr2} = \frac{2\pi}{L}\sqrt{EI_yGJ\left[1 + \frac{4\pi^2 EC_w}{GJL^2}\right]} \tag{2.10}$$

where E is the modulus of elasticity of steel, I_y is moment of inertia about the minor axis, G is the shear modulus of elasticity of steel, J is the torsional constant, and C_w is the warping constant. For this example, the numbers of nodes in the input layer, competition layer, and the interpolation layer are 3, 196

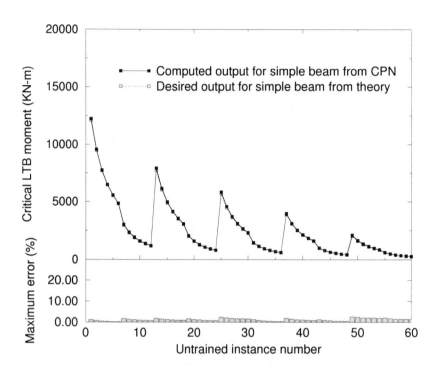

FIGURE 2.6 Learning results for the lateral torsional buckling of simple beams by CPN

(equal to the number of training instances), and 2, respectively (Figure 2.5). This results in a topology with 1176 links, a rather large network. Learning results for the untrained instances are shown in Figures 2.6 and 2.7.   The number of winning nodes in the competition layer was set to four and used for calculating the output of testing instances. For both cases of simply supported and fixed-end beams, the maximum error in critical moments for all sixty verification instances is found to be 2.66%, and 2.46%, respectively. These are within the acceptable limits in design computations.

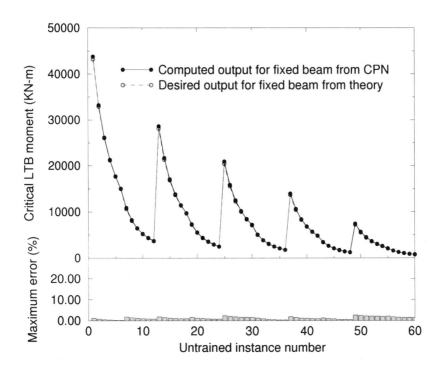

FIGURE 2.7 **Learning results for the lateral torsional buckling of fixed-end beams by CPN**

2.4.2 Moment-gradient coefficient C_b for doubly and singly symmetric steel beams subjected to end moments

The maximum buckling moment, M_{cr}, in a singly symmetric steel beam under nonuniform moments can be approximated by using the moment-gradient coefficient, C_b, as follows (AISC, 1989)

$$M_{cr} = C_b M_{um} \qquad (2.11)$$

where M_{um} is the critical lateral torsional buckling moment of simply supported beams under uniform moment. The coeffi-

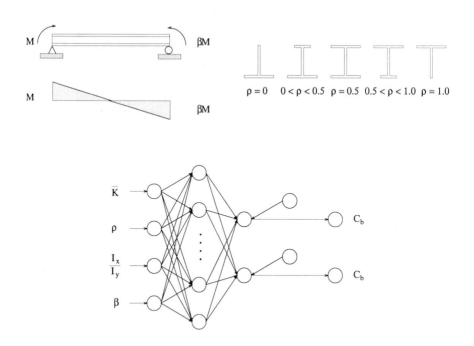

FIGURE 2.8 Counterpropagation for moment-gradient coefficient example

cient, C_b, can be determined only approximately. AISC's ASD specifications (AISC, 1989) recommend the following equation:

$$C_b = 1.75 + 1.05\beta + 0.3\beta^2 \leq 2.3 \qquad (2.12)$$

where $\beta = M_1/M_2$ is the ratio of the two end moments, M_1 being the smaller of the two. This ratio is defined as positive when the end moments cause double curvature deflection, and negative otherwise. The popularity of this equation is due to its simplicity only. This equation is a reasonable approximation for doubly symmetric sections. However, it can be unsafe or overly conservative for monosymmetric beams such as T-sections, especially under a high moment gradient (Kitipornchai et al., 1986).

Kitipornchai et al. (1986) proposed the following complicated equation instead of Eq. (2.12):

$$C_b = \frac{M_{cr}}{M_{um}} = \frac{\gamma_c}{\pi} \left[\sqrt{1 + K^2 + \left(\frac{\pi\delta}{2}\right)^2} + \frac{\pi\delta}{2} \right]^{-1} \qquad (2.13)$$

where γ_c is the nondimensional elastic critical buckling moment, $K = \sqrt{\pi^2 EC_w/GJL_2}$, $\delta = (\beta_x/L)\sqrt{EI_y/GJ}$, and β_x is the monosymmetry parameter ($\beta_x=0$ for doubly symmetric beams). The nondimensional elastic critical buckling moment, γ_c, is computed by the Rayleigh-Ritz method (Chajes, 1974). In this chapter, we include nine terms of the Fourier sine series as the buckled shape function for both lateral deflection and rotation about the longitudinal axis in order to calculate the desired output.

Thus, the counterpropagation network (Figure 2.8) is trained to predict C_b for monosymmetric beams under nonuniform bending. Each training instance for learning this example consists of four nondimensional parameters: the ratio of the moments of inertia of the compression flange and the whole cross-section with respect to the minor axis (ρ), the beam parameter $\bar{K} = \sqrt{\pi^2 EI_y h^2/4GJL^2}$ where h is the distance between flange centroids, the ratio of the moments of inertia of the section about the major and minor axes (I_y/I_x), and the end moment ratio (β). To cover most types of monosymmetric beams, from inverted T shape ($\rho = 0$) to T shape ($\rho = 1.0$), the following combinations of the four parameters are considered as training instances:

$\bar{K}$: { 0.1, 0.5, 1.0, 1.5, 2.0 }

ρ : { 0.0, 0.2, 0.4, 0.6 0.8 1.0 }

I_y/I_x : { 0.005, 0.01 }

β : { -1.0, -0.8, -0.6, -0.4, -0.2, 0.0, 0.2, 0.4, 0.6, 0.8 1.0 }

Thus, the number of training instances is equal to 528. Desired output consists of the two moment-gradient coefficients

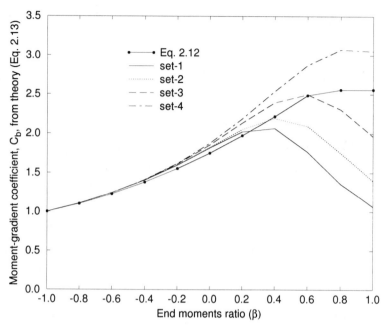

FIGURE 2.9 Desired moment-gradient coefficient value by energy method in Eq. (2.13)

defined by Eqs. (2.12) and (2.13). The numbers of nodes in the input layer, the competition layer, the interpolation layer, and links in the network are 4, 528, 2, and 4224, respectively. The number of winning nodes in the competition layer is set to three for this problem. Forty-four untrained instances were used to test the performance of the network. For all the verification instances, the coefficient, C_b, defined by Eq. (2.12) is predicted with an error of less than 1%. Thus, the results of learning corresponding to Eq. (2.12) are not presented.

The results of learning C_b corresponding to Eq. (2.13) are given in Table 2.4. As the end moment ratio (β) increases, the maximum percentage error for the C_b corresponding to Eq.

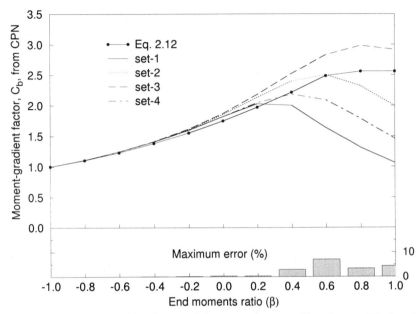

FIGURE 2.10 Prediction of moment-gradient coefficient by the CPN networks

(2.13) generally increases up to 7.1%. Prediction of the moment-gradient coefficient, C_b, for monosymmetric steel beams under nonuniform bending by the counterpropagation is plotted in Figures 2.9 and 2.10.

The forty-four verification instances are divided into four sets depending on the value of the parameter $\bar{K}$ (0.62, 0.74, 1.34, and 1.87). It took 2.77 CPU seconds to train the network, using 528 training instances and testing 44 verification instances. It took 8.09 CPU seconds to determine 572 nondimensional elastic critical buckling moments, γ_c, as training and verification instances by conventional analytical methods on the Cray YMP8/864.

Table 2.4 Learning results for the moment-gradient coefficient corresponding to Eq. (2.13)

Input pattern				Computed output	Desired output	Error (%)
K	ρ	I_y/I_x	β			
0.62	0.93	0.06	-1.0	1.0	1.0	0.00
0.62	0.93	0.06	-0.8	1.11	1.11	0.01
0.62	0.93	0.06	-0.6	1.243	1.242	0.03
0.62	0.93	0.06	-0.4	1.404	1.403	0.08
0.62	0.93	0.06	-0.2	1.599	1.596	0.20
0.62	0.93	0.06	0.0	1.823	1.816	0.39
0.62	0.93	0.06	0.2	2.031	2.022	0.43
0.62	0.93	0.06	0.4	2.004	2.066	2.99
0.62	0.93	0.06	0.6	1.64	1.765	7.08
0.62	0.93	0.06	0.8	1.311	1.357	3.41
0.62	0.93	0.06	1.0	1.061	1.066	0.45
0.74	0.71	0.06	-1.0	1.00	1.0	0.00
0.74	0.71	0.06	-0.8	1.11	1.11	0.00
0.74	0.71	0.06	-0.6	1.244	1.244	0.00
0.74	0.71	0.06	-0.4	1.408	1.408	0.01
0.74	0.71	0.06	-0.2	1.61	1.61	0.03
0.74	0.71	0.06	0.0	1.856	1.855	0.06
0.74	0.71	0.06	0.2	2.136	2.134	0.12
0.74	0.71	0.06	0.4	2.40	2.395	0.21
0.74	0.71	0.06	0.6	2.504	2.499	0.23
0.74	0.71	0.06	0.8	2.323	2.309	0.61
0.74	0.71	0.06	1.0	1.996	1.962	1.73
1.34	0.41	0.08	-1.0	1.0	1.0	0.00
1.34	0.41	0.08	-0.8	1.11	1.11	0.00
1.34	0.41	0.08	-0.6	1.245	1.245	0.00
1.34	0.41	0.08	-0.4	1.41	1.411	0.01
1.34	0.41	0.08	-0.2	1.617	1.617	0.04
1.34	0.41	0.08	0.0	1.873	1.874	0.09
1.34	0.41	0.08	0.2	2.182	2.187	0.22
1.34	0.41	0.08	0.4	2.525	2.593	0.57
1.34	0.41	0.08	0.6	2.833	2.873	1.40
1.34	0.41	0.08	0.8	2.986	3.074	2.88
1.34	0.41	0.08	1.0	2.918	3.053	4.40
1.87	0.77	0.07	-1.0	1.03	1.04	0.00
1.87	0.77	0.07	-0.8	1.11	1.11	0.00
1.87	0.77	0.07	-0.6	1.242	1.242	0.01
1.87	0.77	0.07	-0.4	1.403	1.403	0.01
1.87	0.77	0.07	-0.2	1.597	1.597	0.03
1.87	0.77	0.07	0.0	1.821	1.822	0.08
1.87	0.77	0.07	0.2	2.048	2.052	0.20
1.87	0.77	0.07	0.4	2.187	2.196	0.41
1.87	0.77	0.07	0.6	2.093	2.096	0.15
1.87	0.77	0.07	0.8	1.786	1.753	0.85
1.87	0.77	0.07	1.0	1.458	1.398	4.27

2.5 Conclusions

In this chapter, the counterpropagation neural network algorithm with competition and interpolation layers was presented and applied to several structural engineering examples. The algorithm has been implemented in FORTRAN on the Cray YMP8/864 using the CF77 compiler.

A problem with the backpropagation algorithm is the arbitrary trial-and-error selection of learning and momentum ratios. Similarly, we have the arbitrary trial-and error selection of the learning coefficient, a, in the competition layer and the learning coefficient, b, in the interpolation layer for the conventional counterpropagation algorithm. In this work, we circumvented this problem by using a simple formula as a function of the iteration number for both coefficients and obtained excellent convergence.

The counterpropagation algorithm was compared with the backpropagation algorithm using two examples previously reported in the literature. We found a superior convergence property for the counterpropagation network and a substantial decrease in the CPU time. In one example where the exact data was available, we found the counterpropagation algorithm to be 3000 times faster. The reason for CPN's better convergence property over BPN's is partly due to our definition of the learning coefficient, Eq. (2.4). The superior convergence of the CPN network is also due to the fact that it is less sensitive to the learning coefficients. In BPN, for a given training instance, the weight adjustment process occurs across all connection weights for given learning coefficients. In CPN, however, the weight adjustment process for a given training instance affects only the connection weights associated with the winning node. In BPN, during a training process, a large number of iterations is required for the connection weights to stabilize. For each training instance, a new set of connection weights minimizing the system error must be calculated. In CPN, on the other hand, for each training instance, only the specific connection weights associated with the nodes are to be adjusted.

In addition to the two small neural network examples reported in recent structural engineering literature, we created two large examples with 1176 and 4224 links and 196 and 528 training instances, respectively. The second example is a complex stability analysis problem requiring extensive numerical analysis and management of a large amount of data. In each case the counterpropagation network was trained in less than 30 iterations in both competition and interpolation layers. The verification instances proved the counterpropagation neural network can produce results within a few percentage points of the exact or desirable values and within a reasonable amount of CPU time. Of course, the system error can always be further reduced by additional training.

In a backpropagation neural network, the solution is based on the minimization of the system error. The stabilized weights do not guarantee a global minimum for the system error. In other words, the backpropagation neural network is equivalent to an unconstrained optimization problem. In the counterpropagation algorithm, on the other hand, the specific connection weights associated with a winning node, instead of all connection weights, are adjusted to minimize the error for a given training instance. The learned output from a counterpropagation network is simply the best result from the encoded information based on the given training instances.

As a side result of this research, we found that for monosymmetric thin-walled sections the simple equation in the AISC ASD specification for the moment-gradient coefficient, C_b, is inadequate for moment ratios greater than 0.2. Generally, this error increases with an increase in the moment ratio. While the error is often on the conservative side for many cases, the error is on the nonconservative side for largely monosymmetric beams.

Chapter 3

Neural Dynamics Model for Structural Optimization - Theory

3.1 Introduction

Neural network models inspired by biological nervous systems are providing a new approach to problem solving. Optimization is an area in which the neural network approach has not been used widely. Two different types of optimization problems can be solved using neural networks. The first type is control of mobile robots, where a neural network is used to learn the relationship between sensory input and behavior (Miyamoto et al., 1988). The second type is classical optimization, where a neural network is used to find a node configuration (an equilibrium point) which minimizes an energy or objective function (Tagliarini et al., 1991; Hui and Zåk, 1992).

Hopfield (1982) introduced a Lyapunov energy function (Chetayev, 1961) for the stability of a neural network. This single-layer Hopfield network can operate only on two-state (binary) input and output patterns in discrete time. Cohen and Grossberg (1983) and Hopfield (1984) subsequently developed the single-layer continuous Hopfield network that operates on continuous variables and responses. But, the continuous Hopfield network has a limitation: the connection weights must be symmetric.

Hopfield and Tank (1986) proposed a network for minimizing an energy function by using the differential equation defining the behavior of node activations. They created a network of electrical circuits using continuous-valued units for hardware implementation. In their system, an equilibrium point does not satisfy the Kuhn-Tucker necessary conditions for a local minimum. While their models have been applied to various types of optimization problems, networks converge to invalid solutions which do not satisfy the feasibility and optimality conditions (Jayadeva and Bhaumik, 1992). Kennedy and Chua (1988) developed an analog circuit model based on the nonlinear circuit theory. They studied the stability of an electrical circuit network using a Lyapunov function for the system of differential equations.

While research activity has been reported in the literature on the development of neural network-based optimization algorithms as noted above, no research has been reported on their application to structural optimization problems. We find three characteristics of neural dynamics algorithms attractive in structural optimization problems. They are stability, efficiency, and global convergence.

In this chapter, we formulate a neural dynamics model for structural optimization problems using an exterior penalty function method, and create the corresponding neural network topologies for the dynamic system. In the next chapter we apply the model to the optimum (minimum weight) plastic design of steel frames.

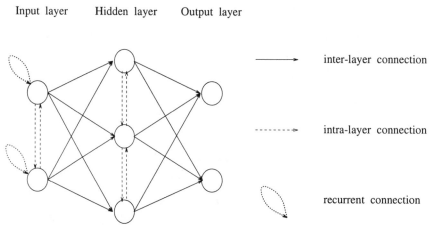

FIGURE 3.1 Topology of an ANN and three connection types

3.2 Artificial Neural Network

An artificial neural network (ANN) is a directed graph composed of nodes and connections between nodes. Generally, an artificial neural network consists of three elements: an organized topology of interconnected nodes (network), a method of encoding information (learning), and a method of recalling information (retrieving).

3.2.1 Topological characteristics

ANN topology consists of layers of nodes linked by weighted interconnections (Figure 3.1). A node has an activation function that evaluates inputs and generates an output as an input to other nodes. A layer that receives inputs from outside of a network is called an input layer and a layer that emits computed output to the environment is an output layer. The layers lying between the input and output layers are called hidden layers.

Characteristics of ANN topologies are described in terms of connection and interconnection types.

1. Connection types. There are two primary connection types: excitatory and inhibitory. An excitatory connection increases the value of input to a connected node and is usually represented by a positive sign. On the other hand, an inhibitory connection decreases the value of input to a connected node and is usually represented by a negative sign.

2. Interconnection types. The three interconnection types are intra-layer (lateral connection), inter-layer, and recurrent connections (Figure 3.1). Intra-layer connections are connections between nodes in the same layer. Inter-layer connections are connections between nodes in different layers. Recurrent connections are direct loops of connections to the same node (Simpson, 1991).

3.2.2   Learning methods

Learning can be defined as any change in the weights to produce some desirable state, and the learning method is a rule that adjusts the weights to the desirable state. Learning methods can be classified into two categories, supervised learning and unsupervised learning.

1. Supervised learning: Learning is performed on the basis of direct comparison of the output of the network with the given desired output. Backpropagation is a widely used

example of supervised learning algorithms (Rumelhart et al., 1986; Adeli and Hung, 1993a & b).

2. Unsupervised learning: The learning goal is not defined. The network is expected to create categories from the correlations of the input data, and to produce output corresponding to the input category. Counterpropagation is an example of unsupervised learning algorithms (Hecht-Neilsen, 1987a & 1988; Adeli and Park, 1995b).

3.2.3 Recalling methods

The recalling method can be defined as the method of finding the corresponding output from the given input after the learning process. The ANN recall mechanisms can be divided in two main categories (Figure 3.2). One is the feedforward recall and the other is the feedback recall mechanism. During the feedforward recall, an input is passed through nodes and weights, and the corresponding output is produced in one pass. In the feedback recall mechanism, an input is passed through the nodes and weights, and then an output is produced which is fed back into an input or a specific layer until there is no change in the weights.

3.3 Neural Dynamics

A system of differential equations defining a dynamic system is defined as

$$\frac{dX_i}{dt} = \dot{X}_i = f_i(X_1, X_2, \cdots, X_n) \tag{3.1}$$

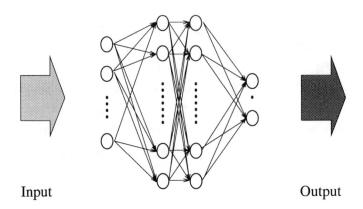

Input   Output

(a) Feedforward Recall

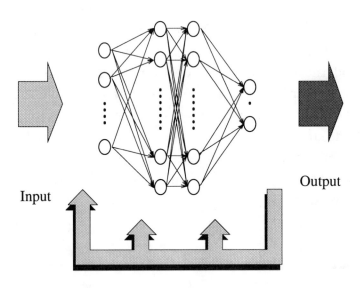

Input   Output

(b) Feedback Recall

FIGURE 3.2 ANN recall mechanism

where $\mathbf{X}(t) = [X_1(t), X_2(t), \cdots, X_n(t)]^T$ represents a vector of time-dependent variables. In general, the rate of change of each variable $X_i(t)$ is a function of $X_i(t)$ itself and all the other variables. A dynamic system is defined as the movement through time of solution trajectories for a system of differential equations. Each trajectory is described by a vector composed of the values of all the variables in the system at any given time. If $f_i(\bar{X}_1, \bar{X}_2, \cdots, \bar{X}_n) = 0$, then a point $\bar{\mathbf{X}}$ is called an equilibrium point of Eq. (3.1).

Now we introduce the important idea of stability of an equilibrium point in a dynamic system. This concept is shown graphically for the case of the three variables in Figure 3.3.

1. Asymptotically Stable: Trajectories starting near the equilibrium point approach the equilibrium point (Figure 3.3a).

2. Stable: Trajectories starting near the equilibrium point stay near the equilibrium point without approaching the equilibrium point (Figure 3.3b).

3. Unstable: Trajectories starting near the equilibrium point move away from the equilibrium point (Figure 3.3c).

We use the Lyapunov function (Hirsch and Smale, 1974) to develop the neural dynamics structural optimization model and prove its stability. The Lyapunov function is defined as a function of the system variables whose values decrease along system trajectories (Chetayev, 1961). Let $V(X_1, X_2, \cdots, X_n)$ be any real-valued continuous function of the state vector $\mathbf{X}$ such that $V(\mathbf{X}) > 0$. Then, if the state vector $\mathbf{X}$ satisfies the system of differential equations (3.1), the chain rule yields

$$\frac{dV}{dt} = \dot{V} = \sum_{i=1}^{n} (\frac{\partial V}{\partial X_i})(\frac{dX_i}{dt}) = \sum_{i=1}^{n} (\frac{\partial V}{\partial X_i}) f_i(\mathbf{X}) \qquad (3.2)$$

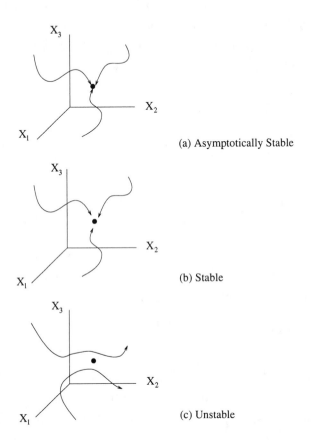

(a) Asymptotically Stable

(b) Stable

(c) Unstable

FIGURE 3.3 Stability of an equilibrium point in a dynamic system

The expression on the right-hand side of Eq. (3.2) is a function of the vector $\mathbf{X}$. The Lyapunov stability theorem states that if $\dot{V} \leq 0$, then the equilibrium point $\bar{X}$ is stable. Also, if $\dot{V} < 0$, then $\bar{X}$ is asymptotically stable (Hirsch and Smale, 1974).

If we can formulate an objective function for the general constrained structural optimization problem in the form of the Lyapunov function, then the Lyapunov stability theorem guarantees that solutions of the corresponding dynamic system (trajectories) for arbitrarily given starting points approach an equilibrium point without increasing the value of the objective function (i.e., the solution is robust). But, this does not guarantee that the equilibrium point is a local minimum. We use the Kuhn-Tucker conditions to verify that the equilibrium point satisfies the necessary condition for a local minimum.

3.4   Kuhn-Tucker Conditions

We can express the nonlinear constrained optimization problem mathematically as follows:

Minimize $F(\mathbf{X})$
subject   to

$$g_j(\mathbf{X}) \leq 0 \quad j = 1, M \tag{3.3}$$

$$h_k(\mathbf{X}) = 0 \quad k = 1, L \tag{3.4}$$

where $g_j(\mathbf{X})$ is the jth inequality constraint function, $h_k(\mathbf{X})$ is the kth equality constraint function, M is the total number of inequality constraints, and L is the total number of the equality constraints. To derive the Kuhn-Tucker conditions for a local minimum, an inequality constraint is transformed to an equality constraint by adding a slack variable, s_j, as follows (Arora, 1989):

$$g_j(\mathbf{X}) + s_j^2 = 0 \tag{3.5}$$

The Lagrange function is defined by combining the objective and constraint functions as follows:

$$L(\mathbf{X}, \mathbf{u}, \mathbf{v}, \mathbf{s}) = F(\mathbf{X}) + \sum_{j=1}^{M} u_j[g_j(\mathbf{X}) + s_j^2] + \sum_{k=1}^{L} v_k h_k(\mathbf{X}) \tag{3.6}$$

where u_j is the Lagrange multiplier for the jth inequality constraint and v_k is the Lagrange multiplier for the kth equality constraint. Then, we find the Lagrangian multipliers u_j^* and v_k^* such that the Lagrangian function becomes stationary with respect to x_i, u_j, v_k, and s_i (Arora,1989),

$$\frac{\partial L}{\partial x_i} = \frac{\partial f}{\partial x_i} + \sum_{j=1}^{M} u_j^* \frac{\partial g_j}{\partial x_i} + \sum_{k=1}^{L} v_k^* \frac{\partial h_k}{\partial x_i} = 0; \quad i = 1, n \tag{3.7}$$

$$g_j(\mathbf{X}^*) + s_j^2 = 0; \quad j = 1, M \tag{3.8}$$

$$h_k(\mathbf{X}^*) = 0; \quad k = 1, L \tag{3.9}$$

$$u_j^* s_j = 0; \quad j = 1, M \tag{3.10}$$

$$u_j^* \geq 0; \quad j = 1, M \tag{3.11}$$

where multipliers v_k^* are unrestricted in sign. For the vector $\mathbf{X}^*$ to be a local optimum solution, the Kuhn-Tucker conditions, Eqs. (3.7) to (3.11), must be satisfied.

3.5 Transformation Methods

The purpose of transformation methods is to transform the general constrained optimization problem to a corresponding unconstrained optimization problem so that an algorithm for the latter can be used for the former. The general approach is to modify the objective function by providing some penalty to limit constraint violations within a given tolerance. To avoid numerical ill-conditioning, only a moderate penalty is provided in the initial optimization stages, and this penalty is increased as the optimization progresses.

The approach to utilizing the penalty function is to create a pseudo-objective function of the form

$$\Psi(\mathbf{X}, r_n) = F(\mathbf{X}) + r_n P(\mathbf{X}) \tag{3.12}$$

where $F(\mathbf{X})$ is the original objective function and $P(\mathbf{X})$ is an imposed penalty function. The scalar, r_n, is a multiplier which determines the magnitude of the penalty. In our neural dynamics model, we use an exterior penalty function in the following form:

$$P(\mathbf{X}) = \sum_{j=1}^{M} \{max[0, g_j(\mathbf{X})]\}^2 + \sum_{k=1}^{L} [h_k(\mathbf{X})]^2 \tag{3.13}$$

If all constraints are satisfied (all $g_j(\mathbf{X}) \le 0$ and all $h_k = 0$), then no penalty is imposed. But, whenever one or more constraints are violated, the square of this constraint is included in the penalty function.

If we choose a small value for r_n, the resulting pseudo-objective function, $\Psi(\mathbf{X}, r_n)$, is easily minimized but may yield major constraint violations. On the other hand, a large value of r_n will ensure near satisfaction of all constraints but will create a poorly conditioned optimization problem from a numerical standpoint. The convergence criteria are that the original function, $F(\mathbf{X})$, does not change significantly during the unconstrained optimization and all constraints are within a specified tolerance.

3.6 Formulation of the Structural Optimization Problem

The structural optimization problem can be cast in the following form:

Minimize

$$\mathbf{W} = \sum_{i=1}^{N} \rho_i A_i L_i \tag{3.14}$$

subject to

$$\sigma_i^L \leq \sigma_{ij} \leq \sigma_i^U \qquad i = 1, N \quad j = 1, N_L \tag{3.15}$$

$$d_{ik}^L \leq d_{ijk} \leq d_{ik}^U \qquad i = 1, N_N \quad j = 1, N_L \quad k = 1, N_D \tag{3.16}$$

$$A_i^L \leq A_i \leq A_i^U \qquad i = 1, N \tag{3.17}$$

where W is the objective function represented by the weight of the structure, ρ_i is the mass density of the *ith* member, L_i is the length of the *ith* member, A_i is the cross-sectional area of the *ith* element, N is the total number of the elements, N_N is the number of nodes, N_L is the number of loading conditions on the structure, and N_D is the number of constrained degrees of freedoms. The constants σ_i^L, σ_i^U, d_{ik}^L, d_{ik}^U, A_i^L, and A_i^U are the lower and upper bounds on the member stresses, nodal displacements, and cross-sectional areas, respectively. Structures are analyzed using the popular finite element method. With a given vector of initial design variables, $\mathbf{X}$, we can assemble the structure stiffness matrix, $\mathbf{K}$, directly from the element stiffness matrices, $\mathbf{k}_i$. The element stiffness matrix, $\mathbf{k}_i$, is calculated from the stiffness matrix, $\mathbf{k}_i^0$, in the local coordinates system and the geometric transformation matrix, $\mathbf{T}$.

$$\mathbf{k}_i = \mathbf{T}^T \mathbf{k}_i^0 \mathbf{T} \tag{3.18}$$

Using the assembled structure stiffness matrix, $\mathbf{K}$, and the assembled nodal load vector, $\mathbf{P}$, the nodal displacements vector, $\mathbf{D}$, can be obtained from

$$\mathbf{K}\mathbf{D} = \mathbf{P} \tag{3.19}$$

Having calculated the nodal displacements, $\mathbf{D}$, we can obtain the internal forces for the *ith* element, $\mathbf{f}_i$,

$$\mathbf{d}_i^0 = \mathbf{T}\mathbf{d}_i \tag{3.20}$$

$$\mathbf{f}_i = \mathbf{k}_i^0 \mathbf{d}_i^0 \tag{3.21}$$

where $\mathbf{d}_i$ and $\mathbf{d}_i^0$ are the displacement vectors for the *ith* element in the global and local coordinate systems, respectively. Finally, from these forces the stresses, σ_i, are calculated and the corresponding constraints are evaluated.

3.7   A Neural Dynamics Model for Structural Optimization

We present a neural dynamics model for structural optimization by integrating the penalty function method, Kuhn-Tucker conditions, Lyapunov's stability theorem, and the neural dynamics concept.

3.7.1   Dynamic system

The general constrained optimization problem defined in Section 3.4 can be formulated as an energy functional to be minimized using the exterior penalty function,

$$V(\mathbf{X}, r_n) = F(\mathbf{X}) + \frac{r_n}{2} \{ \sum_{j=1}^{M} [g_j^+(\mathbf{X})]^2 + \sum_{k=1}^{L} [h_k(\mathbf{X})]^2 \} \quad (3.22)$$

where $g_j^+(\mathbf{X}) = max\{0, g_j(\mathbf{X})\}$ and r_n is the penalty parameter. We define the penalty parameter as a function of the iteration number

$$r_n = r_0 + \frac{n}{\alpha} \quad (3.23)$$

where n is the iteration number, r_0 is the initial penalty parameter, and α is a positive real number whose value depends on optimization problems. In structural optimization problems objective functions are usually positive and continuous, and the second term of the right-hand side of the energy functional, Eq. (3.22), is also positive and continuous. Thus, $V(\mathbf{X}, r_n)$ is a positive and continuous functional and can be treated as a Lyapunov function. To satisfy the Lyapunov stability theorem, however, the derivative of the energy functional with respect to time,

$\dot{V}(\mathbf{X}, r_n)$, must be less than or equal to zero. Taking the derivative of the energy functional $V(\mathbf{X}, r_n)$ with respect to time, we find

$$\frac{dV}{dt} = \dot{V} = \{\frac{\partial F(\mathbf{X})}{\partial \mathbf{X}} + r_n[\sum_{j=1}^{M} g_j^+(\mathbf{X})\frac{\partial g_j}{\partial \mathbf{X}}$$

$$+ \sum_{k=1}^{L} h_k(\mathbf{X})\frac{\partial h(\mathbf{X})}{\partial \mathbf{X}}]\}(\frac{d\mathbf{X}}{dt})$$

$$= \{\nabla F(\mathbf{X}) + r_n[\sum_{j=1}^{M} g_j^+(\mathbf{X})\nabla g_j(\mathbf{X})$$

$$+ \sum_{k=1}^{L} h_k(\mathbf{X})\nabla h_k(\mathbf{X})]\}\dot{\mathbf{X}} \qquad (3.24)$$

where $\nabla F(\mathbf{X})$, $\nabla g_j(\mathbf{X})$, and $\nabla h_k(\mathbf{X})$ are the gradient vectors of the objective function, *jth* inequality constraint function, and *kth* equality constraint function, respectively. For the dynamic system to satisfy the Lyapunov stability theorem, we define

$$\dot{\mathbf{X}} = -\nabla F(\mathbf{X}) - r_n\{\sum_{j=1}^{M} g_j^+\nabla g_j(\mathbf{X}) + \sum_{k=1}^{L} h_k\nabla h_k(\mathbf{X})\} \quad (3.25)$$

Eq. (3.25) is the system of differential equations defining the neural dynamics model for structural optimization. This is, in fact, the learning rule in our ANN model. Now, substituting for $\dot{\mathbf{X}}$ from Eq. (3.25) into Eq. (3.24), we find the derivative of $V(\mathbf{X}, r_n)$ with respect to time:

$$\frac{dV}{dt} = \dot{V}$$

$$= -\ |\ \nabla F(\mathbf{X}) + r_n [\sum_{j=1}^{M} g_j^+(\mathbf{X})\nabla g_j(\mathbf{X})$$

$$+ \sum_{k=1}^{L} h_k(\mathbf{X})\nabla h_k(\mathbf{X})]\ |^2 \le 0 \qquad (3.26)$$

Therefore, the dynamic system always evolves such that the value of the objective function in the original structural optimization problem does not increase. This proves the stability of the dynamic system. In other words, our neural dynamics model for structural optimization problems guarantees global convergence and robustness. An equilibrium point $\bar{\mathbf{X}}$ of the dynamic system can be found by setting Eq. (3.25) equal to zero:

$$\dot{\mathbf{X}} = 0 \qquad (3.27)$$

This equilibrium point $\bar{\mathbf{X}}$ is a design solution of the structural optimization problem and is found by numerical integration:

$$\mathbf{X} = \int \dot{\mathbf{X}} dt \qquad (3.28)$$

The fourth-order Runge-Kutta method (Press et al., 1986) is used for the numerical integration of Eq. (3.28). Also, this point satisfies the Kuhn-Tucker necessary conditions of Eq. (3.7) in which

$$u_j^* = r_n g_j^+(\bar{\mathbf{X}}) \qquad (3.29)$$

and

$$v_k^* = r_n h_k(\bar{\mathbf{X}}) \qquad (3.30)$$

Thus, the equilibrium point of the system is an optimum solution of the structural optimization problem.

3.7.2 Topological characteristics

The neural network in our neural dynamics model consists of two distinct layers: variable and constraint. The number of nodes in the variable layer corresponds to the number of design variables in the structural optimization problem. The number of nodes in the constraint layer is equal to the total number of constraints imposed on the structure. Figure 3.4 shows the topology of the neural dynamics model.

Both excitatory and inhibitory connection types are used for adjusting the states of the nodes. Gradient information about the objective function represented by the first term on the right-hand side of Eq. (3.25) is assigned to the inhibitory recurrent connections in the variable layer. Gradient information for the constraint functions is assigned to the inhibitory connections from the constraint layer to the variable layer. Also, coefficients of the constraint functions are assigned to the excitatory connections from the variable layer to the constraint layer in order to calculate the magnitudes of constraint violations.

Let I_{vi} and O_{vi} be the input and output of the ith node in the variable layer. The anatomy of the functions of the nodes in the variable and constraint layers for our neural dynamics model is presented in Figure 3.5. Input to the nodes in the variable layer is the negative sum of the ith component of the gradient of the objective function (the direction of the steepest descent at the previous point) and the penalty value.

Thus, I_{vi} represents the ith component of the modified search direction at the previous iteration and is found from:

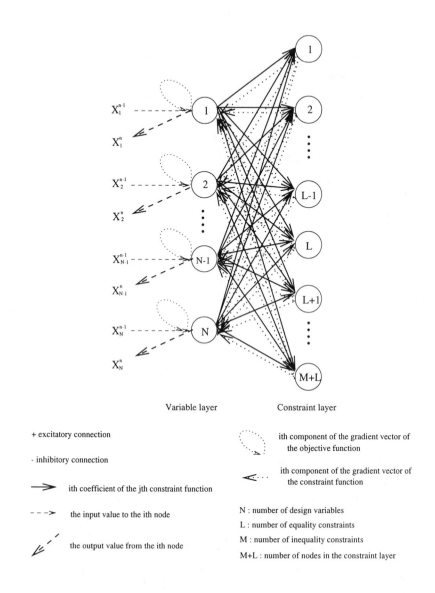

Variable layer   Constraint layer

+ excitatory connection

- inhibitory connection

⟶   ith coefficient of the jth constraint function

- - -➤   the input value to the ith node

↙   the output value from the ith node

⟨⋅⋅⋅   ith component of the gradient vector of
        the objective function

⟨⋅⋅⋅   ith component of the gradient vector of
        the constraint function

N : number of design variables

L : number of equality constraints

M : number of inequality constraints

M+L : number of nodes in the constraint layer

FIGURE 3.4 Topology of neural dynamics model

$$I_{vi} = -\frac{\partial F(\mathbf{X})}{\partial X_i}$$

$$-r_n\{\sum_{j=1}^{M} g_j^+(\mathbf{X})\frac{\partial g_j(\mathbf{X})}{\partial X_i} + \sum_{k=1}^{L} h_k(\mathbf{X})\frac{\partial h_k(\mathbf{X})}{\partial X_i}\} \quad (3.31)$$

The output, O_{vi}, representing the current state of the design variable, X_i, is obtained from the variable layer at any time. A fourth-order Runge-Kutta method is used to integrate Eq. (3.31).

$$X_i = O_{vi} = \int I_{vi} dt \quad (3.32)$$

Let I_{cj}, and O_{cj} be the input and output of the jth node in the constraint layer. Input to the node in this layer is the current state vector, $\mathbf{X}$, and output is the penalty due to the jth constraint violation. The jth output O_{cj} is given by

$$O_{cj} = r_n max\{0, g_j(\mathbf{X})\}; \quad for\ inequality\ constraints \quad (3.33)$$

$$O_{cj} = r_n h_j(\mathbf{X}); \quad for\ equality\ constraints \quad (3.34)$$

If the current state vector, $\mathbf{X}$, from Eq. (3.32), satisfies the jth constraint ($O_{cj} = 0$), there is no activation at the jth node in the constraint layer. Otherwise ($O_{cj} \neq 0$), the value of O_{cj} is fed back to the variable layer in order to modify the search direction to satisfy the jth constraint. Thus, these outputs will be fed back to the corresponding nodes in the variable layer until all the outputs are within the specified tolerance. The dynamic system represented by Eq. (3.25) evolves toward an equilibrium state as the neural network operates in the feedback mechanism. The convergence criteria are that the change in the original objective function be within a specified tolerance and the state vector of design variables from Eq. (3.32) satisfies all the constraints within the given tolerance.

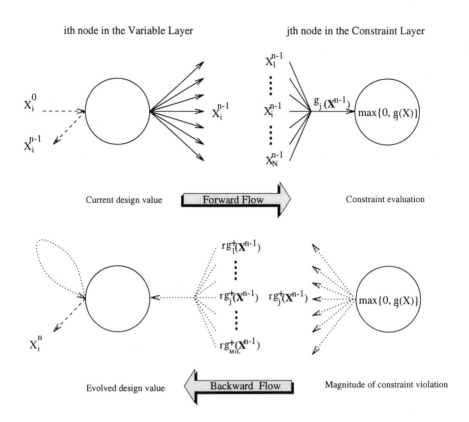

FIGURE 3.5 Anatomy of activation functions

3.8   Conclusions

A neural dynamic model for structural optimization was developed by integrating the penalty function method, Lyapunov's stability theorem, the Kuhn-Tucker conditions, and the neural dynamics concept.

As a significant property of our neural dynamics model for

structural optimization, global convergence of the dynamic system is guaranteed by satisfying the Lyapunov stability theorem. In addition to global convergence, the robustness of the neural dynamics model is achieved by expressing the cost (weight) and constraint functions in the form of the Lyapunov function and setting the penalty parameter as a function of the iteration number. Another attractive characteristic of the proposed neural dynamics model for structural optimization is that it lends itself to effective concurrent processing on high-performance computers (Adeli, 1992a & b). This aspect of the model will be further discussed in subsequent chapters. In the next chapter, the neural dynamics model presented in this chapter is applied to optimum plastic design of steel structures.

Chapter 4

Application of the Neural Dynamics Model to the Plastic Design of Structures

4.1 Introduction

In Chapter 3 we presented a neural dynamics model for the optimization of structures by integrating the penalty function method, Lyapunov's stability theorem, the Kuhn-Tucker conditions, and the neural dynamics concept. In this chapter, we apply the model to the optimum plastic design of low-rise steel frames. The objective and constraint functions are scaled to improve the efficiency and numerical conditioning of the algorithm.

4.2   Computer-Aided Plastic Analysis and Design

Adeli and Mabrouk (1986) present an algorithm for the optimal plastic design of low-rise unbraced frames of general configuration. The algorithm is based on the static approach of limit analysis without generating independent mechanisms. Using the kinematic approach with automatic generation of independent mechanisms, Adeli and Chyou (1986) present an efficient procedure for plastic analysis of irregular low-rise unbraced frames. Adeli and Chyou (1987) present an efficient procedure for optimal plastic design of low-rise frames of general configuration.

We define an objective (weight) function by assuming a linear relationship between the weight per unit length of each member and its plastic moment capacity as follows:

$$W = \sum_{i=1}^{K} L_i M_{pi} \tag{4.1}$$

where M_{pi} is the plastic moment capacity of a group of members i, L_i is the total length of all members associated with group i, and K is the total number of groups. Let J be the number of possible plastic hinge locations and I be the degree of static indeterminacy of the structure. Then, the number of independent failure mechanisms will be

$$H = J - I \tag{4.2}$$

Using the equilibrium method of plastic analysis, we find H independent equilibrium equations resulting in the following H equality constraints:

$$\mathbf{CM} = \mathbf{P} \tag{4.3}$$

where $\mathbf{M}$ is a column vector of moments $M_j(j = 1, \cdots, J)$, $\mathbf{P}$ is a column vector of loads representing the ultimate loads P_u, and $\mathbf{C}$ is an H by J matrix whose elements depend only on the undeformed geometry of the structure.

The moments M_j must satisfy the following plastic moment conditions:

$$-M_{pi} \leq M_j \leq M_{pi} \tag{4.4}$$

$$M_{pi} \geq 0 \tag{4.5}$$

where $i = 1, \cdots, K$ and $j = 1, \cdots, J$. Thus, we have $2J + K$ inequality constraints. We define design variables as the vector $\mathbf{X} = [M_1, \cdots, M_J, M_{p1}, \cdots, M_{pK}]^T$. Then, the objective function is expressed by

$$W(\mathbf{X}) = [0, \cdots, 0, L_1, \cdots, L_K]\mathbf{X} \tag{4.6}$$

Thus, we have the following constrained optimization problem:

Minimize $\quad W(\mathbf{X})$
subject to

$$g_i(\mathbf{X}) = \sum_{j=1}^{J} C_{ij}M_j - P_i = 0 \quad i = 1, \cdots, H \; j = 1, \cdots, J \tag{4.7}$$

$$h_j^{(1)}(\mathbf{X}) = M_j - M_{pi} \leq 0 \quad j = 1, \cdots, J \tag{4.8}$$

$$h_j^{(2)}(\mathbf{X}) = -M_j - M_{pi} \leq 0 \quad j = 1, \cdots, J \tag{4.9}$$

$$h_k^{(3)}(\mathbf{X}) = -M_{pk} \leq 0 \quad k = 1, \cdots, K \tag{4.10}$$

4.3   Application of the Neural Dynamics Model

Before formulating the energy functional to be minimized, the objective and constraint functions are scaled to enhance the efficiency and to improve the conditioning of the optimization process. We normalize coefficients of the objective function, L_i, and scale the design variables, M_i and M_{pi}, as follows

$$\tilde{L}_i = \frac{L_i}{\sum_{j=1}^{K} L_j} \tag{4.11}$$

$$\tilde{M}_i = \frac{M_i}{\sum_{j=1}^{H} P_j} \tag{4.12}$$

$$\tilde{M}_{pi} = \frac{M_{pi}}{\sum_{j=1}^{H} P_j} \tag{4.13}$$

Then, the vector of scaled design variables becomes

$$\tilde{\mathbf{X}} = [\tilde{M}_1, \cdots, \tilde{M}_J, \tilde{M}_{p1}, \cdots, \tilde{M}_{pK}]^T \tag{4.14}$$

Thus, the optimization problem with the scaled objective and constraint functions is defined as follows:

Minimize $W(\tilde{\mathbf{X}}) = [0, \cdots, 0, \tilde{L}_1, \cdots, \tilde{L}_K]\tilde{\mathbf{X}}$
subject to

$$g_i(\tilde{\mathbf{X}}) = \sum_{j=1}^{J} C_{ij} \tilde{M}_j - \frac{P_i}{\sum_{k=1}^{H} P_k} = 0$$
$$i = 1, \cdots, H \quad j = 1, \cdots, J \tag{4.15}$$

$$h_j^{(1)}(\tilde{\mathbf{X}}) = \tilde{M}_j - \tilde{M}_{pi} \leq 0 \quad j = 1, \cdots, J \tag{4.16}$$

$$h_j^{(2)}(\tilde{\mathbf{X}}) = -\tilde{M}_j - \tilde{M}_{pi} \leq 0 \quad j = 1, \cdots, J \tag{4.17}$$

$$h_k^{(3)}(\tilde{\mathbf{X}}) = -\tilde{M}_{pk} \leq 0 \qquad k = 1, \cdots, K \tag{4.18}$$

By this scaling, the values of coefficients are compressed to a small range. This diminishes the possibility of ill-conditioning and accelerates the search process. Now, we formulate the following energy functional (Lyapunov function) to be minimized using the exterior penalty function method:

$$L(\tilde{\mathbf{X}}, r_n) = W(\tilde{\mathbf{X}}) + \frac{r_n}{2}\{\sum_{i=1}^{H}[g_i(\tilde{\mathbf{X}})]^2 + \sum_{j=1}^{J}[h_j^{(1)}(\tilde{\mathbf{X}})]^2$$

$$+ \sum_{j=1}^{J}[h_j^{(2)}(\tilde{\mathbf{X}})]^2 + \sum_{k=1}^{K}[h_k^{(3)}(\tilde{\mathbf{X}})]^2\} \tag{4.19}$$

Consequently, we have the following dynamic system of equations for the optimum plastic design of steel frames that satisfies the Lyapunov stability theorem (Adeli and Park, 1995a):

$$\dot{\tilde{\mathbf{X}}} = -\nabla W(\tilde{\mathbf{X}}) - r_n\{\sum_{i=1}^{H} g_i^+ \nabla g_i(\tilde{\mathbf{X}}) + \sum_{j=1}^{J} h_j^{(1)} \nabla h_j^{(1)}(\tilde{\mathbf{X}})$$

$$+ \sum_{j=1}^{J} h_j^{(2)} \nabla h_j^{(2)}(\tilde{\mathbf{X}}) + \sum_{k=1}^{K} h_k^{(3)} \nabla h_k^{(3)}(\tilde{\mathbf{X}})\} \tag{4.20}$$

The optimum design solution is found by the numerical integration:

$$\tilde{\mathbf{X}}^n = \tilde{\mathbf{X}}^{n-1} + \int \dot{\tilde{\mathbf{X}}}^{n-1} dt \tag{4.21}$$

For implementation of the neural dynamics model, we begin with an arbitrary selection of a starting point (initial design). Since we are using an exterior penalty function method, the starting point does not have to be a feasible design. A large value for the initial penalty parameter can cause numerical ill-conditioning. To circumvent this problem, a relatively small value is initially selected for the penalty parameter. In subsequent iterations, the value of the penalty parameter is increased as a function of the iteration number. Thus, the value of the penalty parameter is updated automatically and a trial-and-error approach for the selection of this parameter is avoided.

The initial values of design variables are fed forward to the constraint layer and constraints are evaluated. Each node in the constraint layer represents a design constraint. Thus, the nodes in the constraint layer fall into two groups. The nodes in the first group are those whose constraints are violated at a given iteration. Outputs of these nodes are the magnitude of the constraint violation multiplied by the penalty parameter. The second group consists of active nodes whose constraints are satisfied with equality within a tolerance (falling on the boundary of the feasible region) and inactive nodes whose constraints are satisfied with inequality (falling within the boundary of the feasible region). The nodes in this group produce a zero output. The outputs from the nodes in the first group of the constraint layer are fed back to the nodes in the variable layer. Since the weight value assigned to the inhibitory connection from the constraint layer to the variable layer is the gradient information of the constraint functions, the input to the nodes in the variable layer is the modified search direction at the given design values.

The outputs from the variable layer are the improved design values based on the previous iteration and calculated by solving the system of differential equations defining the neural dynamics model (Eq. 4.20) using the Runge-Kutta method. As the final step of each iteration the objective function is evaluated based on the improved design values. This process is continued until the stopping criteria or the maximum number of iterations are satisfied.

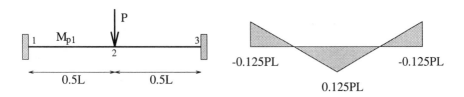

FIGURE 4.1 Fixed-end beam

To demonstrate the behavior of the neural dynamics model, consider a simple example: optimal plastic design of a fixed-end beam subjected to a concentrated load at the midspan. Geometry and properties of the beam as well as the optimal solution are shown in Figure 4.1.

Due to the symmetry of the geometry and loading condition ($M_1 = M_3$), the vector of design variables is

$$\mathbf{X} = [M_1, M_2, M_{p1}]^T \tag{4.22}$$

Thus, the behavior of this problem can be visualized in a three-dimensional design space. We have the following optimization problem with one equality and five inequality constraints:

Minimize $W(\mathbf{X}) = [0, 0, L]\mathbf{X}$
subject to

$$g_1(\mathbf{X}) = -M_1 + M_2 = \frac{PL}{4} \tag{4.23}$$

$$h_1^{(1)}(\mathbf{X}) = M_1 - M_{p1} \leq 0 \tag{4.24}$$

$$h_2^{(1)}(\mathbf{X}) = M_2 - M_{p1} \leq 0 \tag{4.25}$$

$$h_1^{(2)}(\mathbf{X}) = -M_1 + M_{p1} \leq 0 \tag{4.26}$$

$$h_2^{(2)}(\mathbf{X}) = -M_2 + M_{p1} \leq 0 \tag{4.27}$$

$$h_1^{(3)}(\mathbf{X}) = -M_{p1} \leq 0 \tag{4.28}$$

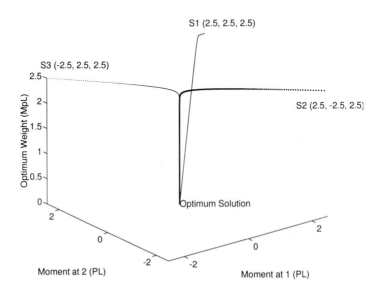

FIGURE 4.2 Solution trajectories for the fixed-end beam

The optimal solution as shown in Figure 4.1 is $\bar{\mathbf{X}} = [-0.125PL,\ 0.125PL,\ 0.125PL^2]^T$. From the neural dynamics model, the solution trajectories using three different starting points are shown in Figures 4.2 and 4.3 which demonstrate that the trajectories converge to the same equilibrium point no matter where they start. Optimum solutions from the neural dynamics model from these starting points are given in Table 4.1.

We observe that the value of the objective function always decreases until the system reaches the optimum solution. This shows the stability and robustness of the neural dynamics model.

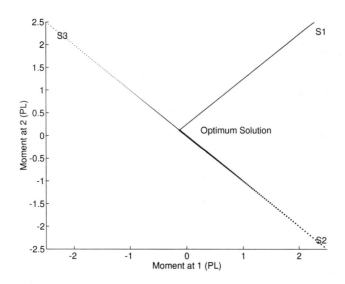

FIGURE 4.3 Equilibrium point for the fixed-end beam

Table 4.1 Equilibrium points from the neural dynamics model for the fixed-beam problem

	Starting point			Equilibrium point		
	M_1 (PL)	M_2 (PL)	M_{p1} (PL^2)	M_1 (PL)	M_2 (PL)	M_{p1} (PL^2)
S1	2.5	2.5	2.5	-0.123	0.123	0.120
S2	- 2.5	2.5	2.5	-0.125	0.125	0.127
S3	2.5	-2.5	2.5	-0.125	0.125	0.128

4.4   Examples

To illustrate the performance of the neural dynamics model, we use four different examples solved previously by Cohn et al. (1972), Adeli and Mabrouk (1986), and Adeli and Chyou (1986 and 1987). The number of independent failure mechanisms (H), number of possible plastic hinge locations (J), number of different groups of members (K), number of design variables, number of equality constraints, and number of inequality constraints for each example are summarized in Table 4.2.

Table 4.2   Data for Examples

	H	J	K	No. of variables	No. of equality constraints	No. of inequality constraints
Example 1	8	14	4	18	8	32
Example 2	10	19	3	22	10	41
Example 3	10	15	4	19	10	34
Example 4	20	38	8	46	20	84

4.4.1   Example 1

The geometry and properties of the frame, as well as the loading system acting on the frame, are shown in Figure 4.4. The number of nodes in the variable and constraint layers are 18 and 46, respectively. The topology of the neural dynamics model is presented in Figure 4.5.

The optimum design solutions from the neural dynamics model and Adeli and Chyou (1987) are given in Table 4.3. Figure 4.6 shows the convergence history for this example using different starting points. This figure demonstrates the global convergence and stability of the neural dynamics model.

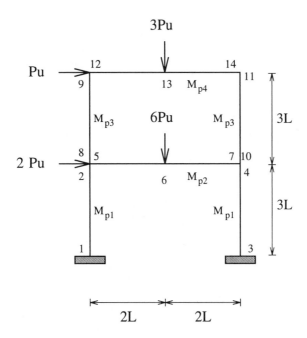

FIGURE 4.4 Example 1 (possible plastic hinge locations are numbered in the figure)

Table 4.3   Optimum solutions for Example 1

	Optimum weight	Optimum solutions (PL)			
	W (PL^2)	M_{p1}	M_{p2}	M_{p3}	M_{p4}
Adeli and Chyou (1987)	51.00	3.00	4.50	1.50	1.50
Neural Dynamics	51.04	2.97	4.46	1.49	1.61

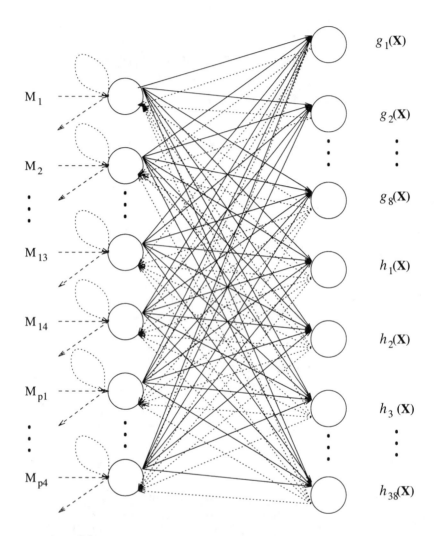

FIGURE 4.5 The topology of the neural dynamics model for Example 1

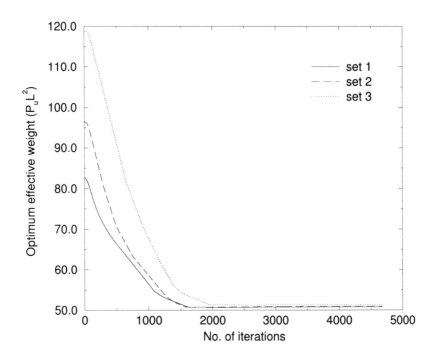

FIGURE 4.6 Convergence history for Example 1

4.4.2 Example 2

This example is a two-story, two-bay unsymmetric frame. The geometry and properties of this frame, as well as the loading system acting on the frame, are shown in Figure 4.7. The number of nodes in the variable and constraint layers are 22 and 51, respectively. The optimum design solutions from the neural dynamics model and Adeli and Chyou (1987) are given in Table 4.4. Figure 4.8 shows the convergence history for this example using different three starting points.

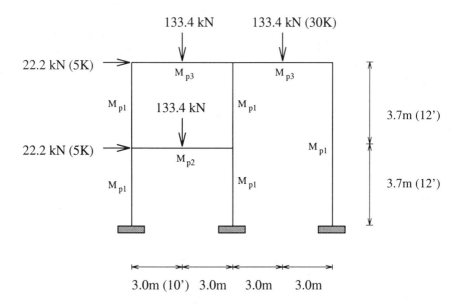

FIGURE 4.7 Example 2

Table 4.4   Optimum solutions for Example 2

	Optimum weight kNm^2 $(kip-ft^2)$	Optimum solutions, kNm $(kip-ft)$		
		M_{p1}	M_{p2}	M_{p3}
Adeli and Chyou	3380.93 (8167.27)	51.82	103.64	132.02
(1987)		(38.18)	(76.36)	(97.27)
Neural Dynamics	3392.87 (8196.08)	53.39	107.47	128.26
		(39.34)	(79.18)	(94.50)

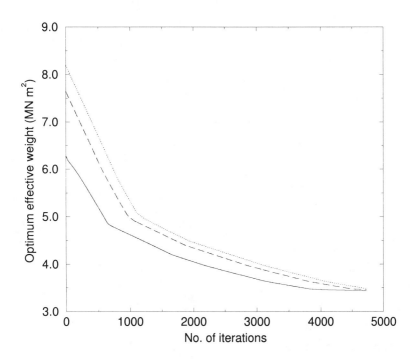

FIGURE 4.8 Convergence history for Example 2

4.4.3 Example 3

This example is a two-story frame with inclined members as shown in Figure 4.9. The number of nodes in the variable and constraint layers are 19 and 44, respectively. The optimum design solutions from the neural dynamics model and Adeli and Mabrouk (1986) are given in Table 4.5. Figure 4.10 shows the convergence history for this example using three different starting points.

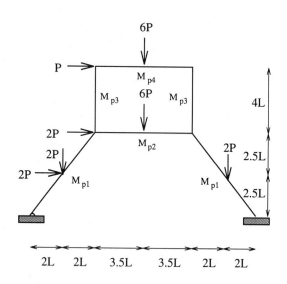

FIGURE 4.9 Example 3

Table 4.5   Optimum solutions for Example 3

	Optimum weight W (PL^2)	Optimum solutions (PL)			
		M_{p1}	M_{p2}	M_{p3}	M_{p4}
Adeli and Mabrouk (1986)	127.45	4.19	6.59	2.40	2.50
Neural Dynamics	127.91	4.47	6.59	2.10	2.33

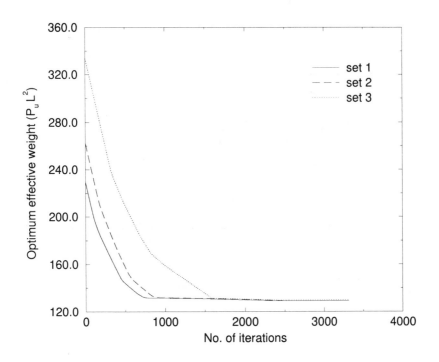

FIGURE 4.10 Convergence history for Example 3

4.4.4 Example 4

This example is a four-story irregular frame shown in Figure 4.11. The number of nodes in the variable and constraint layers are 46 and 104, respectively. The optimum design solutions from the neural dynamics model and Adeli and Mabrouk (1986) are given in Table 4.6. Figure 4.12 shows the convergence history for this example using different starting points. Figures 4.13 and 4.14 show the CPU time on an IBM 3090-600/J for Examples 1 to 4 as functions of the total number of design variables and constraints, respectively.

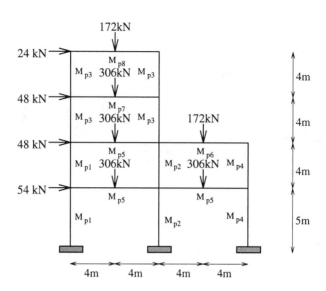

FIGURE 4.11 Example 4

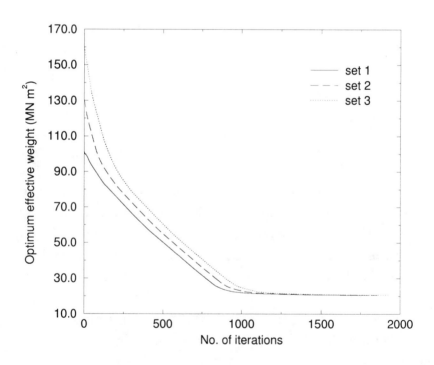

FIGURE 4.12 Convergence history for Example 4

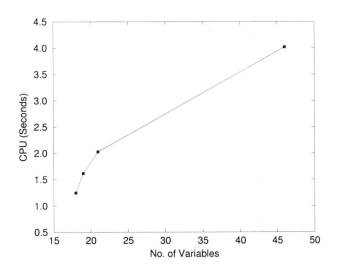

FIGURE 4.13 CPU times for various examples as a function of the number of variables

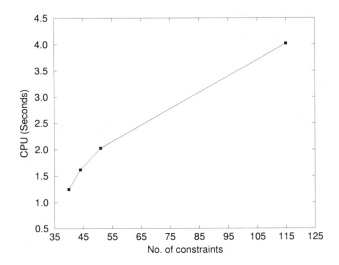

FIGURE 4.14 CPU times for various examples as a function of the number of constraints

Table 4.6   Optimum solutions for Example 4

Optimum Solutions (kNm)	Adeli and Mabrouk (1986)	Neural Dynamics
M_{p1}	64.63	61.46
M_{p2}	185.19	173.16
M_{p3}	173.82	78.72
M_{p4}	199.30	199.41
M_{p5}	398.60	378.35
M_{p6}	172.00	212.72
M_{p7}	347.63	518.40
M_{p8}	173.82	244.43
Optimum weight (kNm^2)	21936.82	22050.00

4.5   Conclusion

In this chapter we applied the neural dynamics model developed to the optimum plastic design of low-rise steel structures. As demonstrated in the convergence histories for the four examples, the neural dynamics model, based on the integration of an exterior penalty function, Lyapunov's stability theorem, the Kuhn-Tucker conditions, and the neural dynamics concept, yields stable results no matter how the starting point is selected. We formulated the plastic design of low-rise frames as a linear programming problem; but, the neural dynamics model for structural optimization is general and can be applied to nonlinear programming problems also. We are encouraged by the robustness and global convergence of the model. In the following chapters we will present the application of the neural dynamics model to the optimization of large structures with several hundreds or a few thousand members such as high-rise and superhigh-rise building structures subjected to the constraints of the American Institute of Steel Construction (AISC)'s Allowable Stress Design (AISC, 1989) and Load and Resistance Factor Design (AISC, 1994) specifications. Optimization of such large structures requires substantial computer processing time (Adeli and Kamal, 1993). Since the neural dynamics model lends itself to effective concurrent processing, the development of a concurrent neural dynamics model for the optimization of large structures will be very valuable.

Chapter 5

Nonlinear Neural Dynamics Model for Optimization of Space Structures

5.1 Introduction

Neural dynamics is defined by a system of first-order differential equations governing time evolutionary changes in node (neuron) activations. In general, a neural network consists of a learning rule that controls the changes in the connection weights and a topology of interconnected nodes that evaluate inputs and generate outputs for nodes in the next layer.

In this chapter we present a nonlinear neural dynamics model as an optimization process for space structures subjected to general constraints such as displacement, stress, and side constraints. We formulate a Lyapunov function for general constrained optimization of structures in terms of an exterior penalty function method and construct an appropriate neural network topology for multiple loading conditions. Once we have a Lyapunov function for the optimization problem, the Lyapunov stability theorem guarantees that trajectories of the corresponding dynamic system for any arbitrarily given starting point approach an equilibrium point without increasing the value of the objective function. The equilibrium point represents a local minimum of the optimization problem which satisfies the Kuhn-Tucker conditions.

5.2   Formulation of the Structural Optimization Problem

The structural optimization of space axial-load structures can be cast in the following form:

Minimize

$$F(\mathbf{X}) = \sum_{i}^{M} \rho_i X_i L_i \tag{5.1}$$

Subject to

$$\sigma_i^L \leq \sigma_i^j \leq \sigma_i^U \qquad i = 1, M \quad j = 1, N_L \tag{5.2}$$

$$d_i^L \leq d_i^j \leq d_i^U \qquad i = 1, N \quad j = 1, N_L \tag{5.3}$$

$$X_i^L \leq X_i \leq X_i^U \qquad i = 1, M \tag{5.4}$$

where $F(\mathbf{X})$ is the objective function represented by the weight of the structure, ρ_i is the mass density of the ith member, X_i is the cross-sectional area of the ith member, L_i is the length of the ith member, M is the total number of the elements, N is the number of constrained degrees of freedom, N_L is the number of loading conditions on the structure, and $\sigma_i^L, \sigma i^U, d_i^L, d_i^U, X_i^L$, and X_i^U are the lower and upper bounds on the member stresses, nodal displacements, and cross-sectional areas, respectively. The element stresses and nodal displacements are found by a finite element structural analysis for every loading condition in every iteration.

To formulate a pseudo-objective function for the optimization of space structures in the form of the Lyapunov function, the constrained optimization problem is transformed to an unconstrained problem by an exterior penalty function method (Arora, 1989). The reason for utilizing the penalty function is to modify the objective function by providing some penalty to limit constraint violations within a given tolerance. In this work, we define the following penalty function for optimization of structures:

$$P(\mathbf{X}) = \sum_{j=1}^{M} \{max[0, g_j(\mathbf{X})]\}^2 + \sum_{k=1}^{N} \{max[0, g_k(\mathbf{X})]\}^2 \quad (5.5)$$

where $g_j(\mathbf{X})$ and $g_k(\mathbf{X})$ are the jth normalized stress constraint function and the kth normalized displacement constraint function in the following form:

$$g_j(\mathbf{X}) = \frac{\sigma_j}{\sigma_j^a} - 1 \leq 0 \qquad j = 1, M \qquad (5.6)$$

$$g_k(\mathbf{X}) = \frac{d_k}{d_k^a} - 1 \leq 0 \qquad j = 1, N \qquad (5.7)$$

and

$$
\begin{array}{llll}
\sigma_j^a = \sigma_j^L & if & \sigma_j < 0 \\
\sigma_j^a = \sigma_j^U & if & \sigma_j \geq 0 \\
d_k^a = d_k^L & if & d_k < 0 \\
d_k^a = d_k^U & if & d_k \geq 0 & (5.8)
\end{array}
$$

In the following sections, the subscripts j and k are used to denote stress and displacement constraint functions, respectively.

Now we define the following energy functional as a pseudo-objective function and prove in the next section that it is, in fact, an acceptable Lyapunov function.

$$V(\mathbf{X}, r_n) = F(\mathbf{X}) + \frac{r_n}{2} P(\mathbf{X})$$

$$= F(\mathbf{X}) + \frac{r_n}{2} \left\{ \sum_{j=1}^{M} [g_j^+(\mathbf{X})]^2 + \sum_{k=1}^{N} [g_k^+(\mathbf{X})]^2 \right\} \quad (5.9)$$

where r_n is the penalty coefficient, $g_j^+(\mathbf{X}) = max[0, g_j(\mathbf{X})]$, and $g_k^+(\mathbf{X}) = max[0, g_k(\mathbf{X})]$.

5.3   A Nonlinear Neural Dynamics Model for Structural Optimization

Our nonlinear neural dynamics model for optimization of structures consists of four components: two information flow control components and two information server components. The first component is a neural dynamic system of linear differential equations which corresponds to a learning rule. This governs time evolutionary changes in node activations. The second component is the topology with one variable layer and N_L multiconstraint layers, each corresponding to a loading condition.

The first information server component performs finite element analysis and finds the magnitudes of constraint violations. The other information server finds the design sensitivity coefficients. The schematic functional interaction of various components is shown in Figure 5.1.

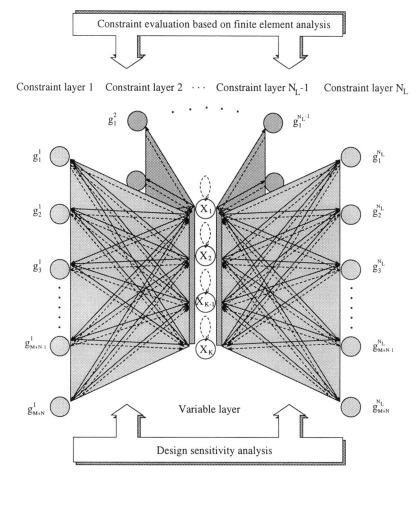

FIGURE 5.1 Functional interaction of components in the neural dynamics model for optimization of structures

5.3.1   Dynamic system

The energy functional, $V(\mathbf{X}, r_n)$, is a positive and continuous functional. To satisfy the Lyapunov stability theorem, the derivative of the energy functional with respect to time, $\dot{V}(\mathbf{X}, r_n)$, must be less than or equal to zero. The derivative of the energy functional $V(\mathbf{X}, r_n)$ with respect to time can be written as

$$
\dot{V} = \left\{ \frac{\partial F(\mathbf{X})}{\partial \mathbf{X}} + r_n \left[\sum_{j=1}^{M} g_j^+(\mathbf{X}) \frac{\partial g_j(\mathbf{X})}{\partial \mathbf{X}} \right. \right.
$$
$$
\left. \left. + \sum_{k=1}^{N} g_k^+(\mathbf{X}) \frac{\partial g_k(\mathbf{X})}{\partial \mathbf{X}} \right] \right\} \left(\frac{d\mathbf{X}}{dt} \right)
$$
$$
= \left\{ \nabla F(\mathbf{X}) + r_n \left[\sum_{j=1}^{M} g_j^+(\mathbf{X}) \nabla g_j(\mathbf{X}) \right. \right.
$$
$$
\left. \left. + \sum_{k=1}^{N} g_k^+(\mathbf{X}) \nabla g_k(\mathbf{X}) \right] \right\} \dot{\mathbf{X}} \tag{5.10}
$$

For the dynamic system to satisfy the Lyapunov stability theorem, we impose the following condition on the design variables:

$$
\dot{\mathbf{X}} = -\nabla F(\mathbf{X}) - r_n \left[\sum_{j=1}^{M} g_j^+(\mathbf{X}) \nabla g_j(\mathbf{X}) \right.
$$
$$
\left. + \sum_{k=1}^{N} g_k^+(\mathbf{X}) \nabla g_k(\mathbf{X}) \right] \tag{5.11}
$$

Substituting for $\dot{\mathbf{X}}$ from Eq. (5.11) into Eq. (5.10), we find the derivative of $V(\mathbf{X}, r_n)$ with respect to time:

$$
\frac{dV}{dt} = \dot{V}
$$
$$
= - \left| \nabla F(\mathbf{X}) + r_n [\sum_{j=1}^{M} g_j^+(\mathbf{X}) \nabla g_j(\mathbf{X}) \right.
$$

$$+ \sum_{k=1}^{N} g_k^+(\mathbf{X})\nabla g_k(\mathbf{X})] \mid^2 \leq 0 \qquad (5.12)$$

Eq. (5.11) is the system of differential equations defining the neural dynamics model for structural optimization. From Eq. (5.12) we find an important characteristic of our neural dynamics model:

> If $\dot{\mathbf{X}} \neq 0$, then $\dot{V} < 0$ and V will always decrease.

> If $\dot{\mathbf{X}} = 0$, then $\dot{V} = 0$ and V will not change.

Therefore, the dynamic system always evolves such that the value of the objective function in the original structural optimization problem does not increase. This proves the stability of the dynamic system and the correctness of Eq. (5.9) as a Lyapunov function. In other words, our neural dynamics model for structural optimization problems guarantees global convergence and robustness. An equilibrium point $\bar{\mathbf{X}}$ of the dynamic system can be found by setting Eq. (5.11) equal to zero:

$$\dot{\bar{\mathbf{X}}} = 0 \qquad (5.13)$$

This equilibrium point $\bar{\mathbf{X}}$ is a design solution of the structural optimization problem and is found by numerical integration:

$$\bar{\mathbf{X}} = \int \dot{\mathbf{X}} dt \qquad (5.14)$$

The Euler method (Press et al., 1986) is used for the numerical integration of Eq. (5.14). Also, this equilibrium point satisfies the Kuhn-Tucker necessary conditions where $r_n g_j^+(\bar{\mathbf{X}})$ and $r_n g_k^+(\bar{\mathbf{X}})$ correspond to the Lagrangian multipliers. Thus, the equilibrium point of the system is an optimum solution of the structural optimization problem.

5.3.2   Topological characteristics

The neural network in our neural dynamics model consists of one variable layer and N_L constraint layers. Each constraint layer represents one loading condition. The number of nodes in the variable layer corresponds to the number of independent design variables (K) in the structural optimization problem. The number of nodes in each constraint layer is equal to the total number of constraints $(M + N)$ imposed on the structure.

Both excitatory and inhibitory connection types are used for adjusting the state of the nodes. Gradient information of the objective function represented by the first term in the right-hand side of Eq. (5.11) is assigned to the inhibitory recurrent connections in the variable layer. The ith recurrent connection weight of the ith node in the variable layer is $C_i = -\partial F(\mathbf{X})/\partial X_i$. Gradient information of the constraint functions shown in the second term in the right-hand side of Eq. (5.11) is assigned to the inhibitory connections from the constraint layer to the variable layer. The weights of the inhibitory connections from the jth and kth nodes in the constraint layer to the ith node in the variable layer are $w_{ji} = -\partial g_j(\mathbf{X})/\partial X_i$ and $w_{ki} = -\partial g_k(\mathbf{X})/\partial X_i$, respectively.

Let I_{cj}^m, and O_{cj}^m be the input and output of the jth node in the mth constraint layer. Each node in the constraint layer represents a design constraint. The initial values of design variables are fed forward to constraint layers and design constraints are evaluated. Thus, the nodes in each constraint layer fall into two groups. The nodes in the first group are those whose constraints are violated at a given iteration. Outputs of these nodes are the magnitudes of the constraints violations multiplied by the penalty parameter:

for stress constraints

$$O_{cj}^m = r_n \, max\{0, g_j^m(\mathbf{X})\} \tag{5.15}$$

for displacement constraints

$$O_{ck}^m = r_n \, max\{0, g_k^m(\mathbf{X})\} \tag{5.16}$$

The second group consists of inactive nodes whose constraints are satisfied with inequality (falling within the boundary of the feasible region). The nodes in this group produce a zero output. Outputs from the nodes in the first group of constraint layers, $O_{cj}^m \neq 0$, $m = 1, N_L$, will be fed back to the corresponding nodes in the variable layer.

Let I_{vi}^m be the *ith* input from the *mth* constraint layer and O_{vi} be the output of the *ith* node in the variable layer. Input to the nodes in the variable layer is the negative sum of the *ith* component of the gradient of the objective function (the direction of the steepest descent at the previous point) and the penalty value.

$$I_{vi}^m = C_i + \sum_{j=1}^{M} w_{ji}^m O_{cj}^m + \sum_{k=1}^{N} w_{ki}^m O_{ck}^m$$

$$i = 1, \; K, \;\; j = 1, \; M, \;\; k = 1, \;\; N, \;\; and \;\; m = 1, \; N_L \tag{5.17}$$

Since the weight values assigned to the inhibitory connections from constraint layers to the variable layer are the gradient information of constraint functions, I_{vi}^m is the *ith* component of the modified direction for the *mth* loading condition at the given design value. To satisfy all the imposed constraints on a structure under the multiple loading conditions, there is a competition among I_{vi}^m, $m = 1, N_L$, and the maximum of these values is chosen as the final modified search direction of the variable at the current iteration:

$$I_{vi} = max\{I_{vi}^1, I_{vi}^2, \cdots, I_{vi}^{N_L}\} \quad i = 1, K \qquad (5.18)$$

If I_{vi} is positive, then the value of the *ith* design variable, X_i, will be increased in order to reduce the magnitude of constraint violations. Otherwise, the value of X_i will be decreased. Then, the output, O_{vi}^n, representing the improved value of the *ith* design variable at the *nth* iteration, $\mathbf{X}_i^n$, is calculated by solving the system of differential equations, Eq. (5.11), using the Euler numerical integration method represented by Eq. (5.14):

$$O_{vi}^n = O_{vi}^{n-1} + \int I_{vi} dt \qquad (5.19)$$

In the final stage of each iteration the objective function is evaluated using the improved design variables. This process is continued until the stopping criteria are satisfied or the maximum number of iterations is met. For the stopping criteria, the change in the original objective function should be within a specified tolerance and the design variables should satisfy all the constraints within a given tolerance.

5.3.3   Sensitivity analysis

In the linear neural dynamics model for structural optimization where the constraints are linear functions of design variables, the gradients of the constraints do not depend upon design variables. However, in the nonlinear neural dynamics model for optimization of structures, the gradient information describing the dependence of structural response such as displacements and stresses on design variables is not constant and depends on design variables. In the nonlinear neural dynamics model we calculate the derivatives of constraint functions, Eqs (5.6) and (5.7), with respect to design variables by the adjoint variable method (Arora and Haug, 1979) and assign them to the inhibitory connections from the constraint layers to the variable layer (Figure 5.1).

Consider a general *ith* constraint as a function of both vector of design variables, $\mathbf{X}$, and nodal displacement vector, $\mathbf{u}$.

$$g_i = g_i[\mathbf{X}, \mathbf{u}(\mathbf{X})] \leq 0 \tag{5.20}$$

Then, the sensitivity coefficient of the *ith* constraint with respect to the *jth* design variable in the *mth* loading condition is

$$\frac{dg_i}{dX_j} = \frac{dg_i[\mathbf{X}, \mathbf{u}^m(\mathbf{X})]}{dX_j}$$

$$i = 1,\ M+N,\quad j = 1,\ K,\quad and\quad m = 1,\ N_L \tag{5.21}$$

Differentiating Eq. (5.21) by the chain rule, we find

$$\frac{dg_i}{dX_j} = \frac{\partial g_i}{\partial X_j} + \frac{\partial g_i}{\partial u_k^m}\frac{\partial u_k^m}{\partial X_j}$$

$$i = 1,\ M+N,\ j = 1,\ K,\ k = 1,\ N,\ and\ m = 1,\ N_L \tag{5.22}$$

where u_k^m is the nodal displacement for the *kth* constrained degree of freedom due to the *mth* loading condition.

The derivative of displacement with respect to a design variable, $\partial u_k^m/\partial X_j$, is found from the equilibrium equation or a finite element analysis of the structure:

$$\mathbf{K}\mathbf{u}^m = \mathbf{P}^m \tag{5.23}$$

where $\mathbf{K}$ is the assembled structure stiffness matrix and $\mathbf{P}^m$ is the assembled structure nodal load vector for the *mth* loading condition. Differentiation of both sides of Eq. (5.23) with respect to design variable, X_i, yields

$$\mathbf{K}\frac{\partial u_k^m}{\partial X_j} = -\frac{\partial \mathbf{K}}{\partial X_j}\mathbf{u}^m + \frac{\partial \mathbf{P}^m}{\partial X_j} \tag{5.24}$$

or

$$\frac{\partial u_k^m}{\partial X_j} = \mathbf{K}^{-1}\left[-\frac{\partial \mathbf{K}}{\partial X_j}\mathbf{u}^m + \frac{\partial \mathbf{P}^m}{\partial X_j}\right] \tag{5.25}$$

By substituting Eq. (5.25) into Eq.(5.22), we find the sensitivity coefficients:

$$\frac{dg_i}{dX_j} = \frac{\partial g_i}{\partial X_j} + \frac{\partial g_i}{\partial u_k^m}\mathbf{K}^{-1}\left[-\frac{\partial \mathbf{K}}{\partial X_j}\mathbf{u}^m + \frac{\partial \mathbf{P}^m}{\partial X_j}\right]$$

$$i = 1,\ M + N,\ j = 1,\ K,\ k = 1,\ N,\ and\ m = 1,\ N_L \tag{5.26}$$

In order to avoid inverting the structure stiffness matrix, rather than calculating $\partial u_k^m/\partial X_j$ directly from Eq. (5.25), the adjoint variable method is used. The adjoint variable vector of the *ith* constraint is defined as

$$\xi_i^m = \left[\frac{\partial g_i}{\partial u_k^m}\mathbf{K}^{-1}\right]^T = \mathbf{K}^{-1}\left\{\frac{\partial g_i}{\partial u_k^m}\right\}^T \tag{5.27}$$

and is found by solving the following adjoint linear system of equations:

$$\mathbf{K}\xi_i^m = \left\{\frac{\partial g_i}{\partial u_k^m}\right\}^T \tag{5.28}$$

The stiffness matrix $\mathbf{K}$ in Eqs. (5.23) and (5.28) is the same. Thus, the stiffness matrix is factorized only once in each structural analysis stage. Thus, the design sensitivity coefficient for the *ith* constraint and the *mth* loading condition is found from

$$\frac{dg_i}{dX_j} = \frac{\partial g_i}{\partial X_j} + \{\xi_i^m\}^T\left[-\frac{\partial \mathbf{K}}{\partial X_j}\mathbf{u}^m + \frac{\partial \mathbf{P}^m}{\partial X_j}\right]$$

$$i = 1, \ M + N, \ j = 1, \ K, \ k = 1, \ N, \ and \ m = 1, \ N_L \quad (5.29)$$

The sensitivity coefficients shown in Eq. (5.29) are calculated using unlinked design variables. However, a node in the variable layer represents a linked design variable. Thus, the sensitivity coefficients in Eq. (5.29) are also linked similarly to design variables and assigned to appropriate connections. Sensitivity coefficients of the objective and constraint functions with respect to linked variables, X_i, are found from

$$\frac{\partial F(\mathbf{X})}{\partial X_i} = \sum_{j=1}^{D} \frac{\partial F(\mathbf{X})}{\partial Y_j} \frac{\partial Y_j}{\partial X_i} \qquad i = 1, \cdots, K \qquad (5.30)$$

$$\frac{\partial g_i(\mathbf{X})}{\partial X_j} = \sum_{k=1}^{D} \frac{g_i(\mathbf{X})}{\partial Y_k} \frac{\partial Y_k}{\partial X_j} \qquad i = 1, \cdots, M + N \qquad (5.31)$$

where X_i is the *ith* independent (linked) variable, Y_j is the *jth* dependent variable in the *ith* linked variable, and D is the number of dependent variables grouped as the *ith* linked variable. In every iteration, sensitivity coefficients are computed for only active constraints and assigned to the corresponding inhibitory connections from the constraint layers to the variable layer.

5.4 Implementation

In order to improve the efficiency of the optimization process, the original objective and constraint functions are scaled. The objective of this scaling is to limit the possible values for sensitivity coefficients of these functions to a small range of zero to 1. Normalized constraints are given by Eqs. (5.6) and (5.7). Now, we normalize the original objective function as follows:

$$\tilde{F}(\mathbf{X}) = \frac{1}{\sum_{i=1}^{M} \rho_i L_i} F(\mathbf{X}) \qquad (5.32)$$

For implementation of this model, we begin with an arbitrary set of initial values for linked design variables. A relatively small value is initially selected for the penalty parameter. The value of the penalty parameter is increased as a function of the iteration number in subsequent iterations in the following manner:

$$r_n = r_0 + \frac{n}{\alpha} \qquad (5.33)$$

where n is the iteration number, r_0 is the initial penalty parameter, and α is a positive real number whose value depends on the problems being solved. As a stopping criterion, a tolerance of 10^{-5} is used for the original objective function. The maximum number of iterations is set at 80 for all examples. The algorithm presented in this chapter is implemented in FORTRAN on two types of computers: IBM RISC 6000 workstation and Cray YMP8/864 supercomputer.

5.5   Examples

We apply the nonlinear neural dynamics model presented in this chapter to minimum weight design of four example structures. The first three examples are taken from the literature for the sake of comparison. The fourth example is a large structure created in this research. For the first three examples we use the following values for the modulus of elasticity and the unit weight of the material: E=68.95 GPa (10000 ksi) and ρ=27.14 kN/m³ (0.1 lb/in³). The modulus of elasticity and the unit weight of the material for the fourth example are E=198.91 GPa (29000 ksi) and ρ=79.97 kN/m³ (490.0 lb/ft³).

5.5.1 Example 1. 12-bar space truss

This example is a twelve-bar space truss shown in Figure 5.2. The twelve members of the structure are linked to three independent variables, as identified in Table 5.1.

The structure is subjected to two loading conditions as follows:

loading condition 1 : $P_1 = 0$, $P_2 = -266.9$ kN $(-60$ kips)

loading condition 2 : $P_1 = 66.7$ kN (15 kips), $P_2 = 0$

The upper and lower bounds on stress in each member are 137.9 MPa (20 ksi) in tension and -103.4 MPa $(-15$ ksi) in compression. Displacement limits of ±0.635 cm (±0.25 in) and ±1.016 cm (±0.4 in) are imposed at joint 1 in the x and y directions, respectively. The lower bound of cross-sectional areas is given as

Table 5.1 Optimum solutions for Example 1

Variable	Member	Optimum solution, cm^2 (in^2)	
		Adeli and Kamal (1986)	Neural dynamics
1	1, 3, 4	14.9767 (2.2282)	12.6703 (1.9639)
2	2, 5, 6	6.1000 (0.9455)	7.1419 (1.1070)
3	7, 8, 9	9.3103 (1.4431)	8.1264 (1.2596)
	10, 11, 12		
Optimum weight, N (lb)		639.94 (143.64)	617.90 (138.91)

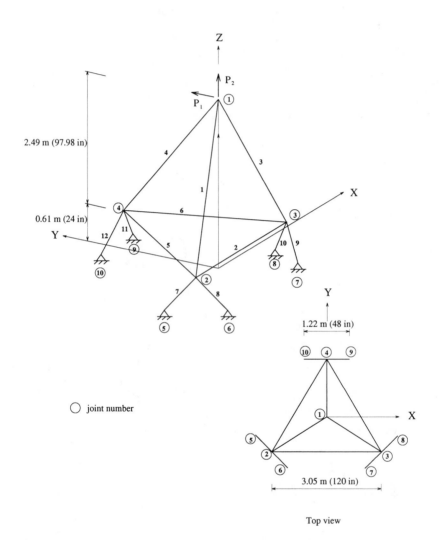

FIGURE 5.2 Twelve-bar space truss

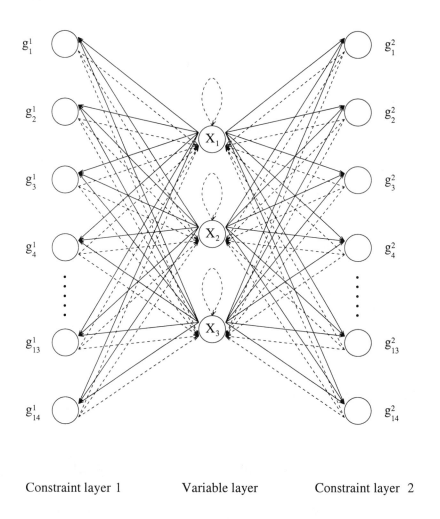

Constraint layer 1   Variable layer   Constraint layer 2

FIGURE 5.3 Topology of the neural dynamics model for Example 1

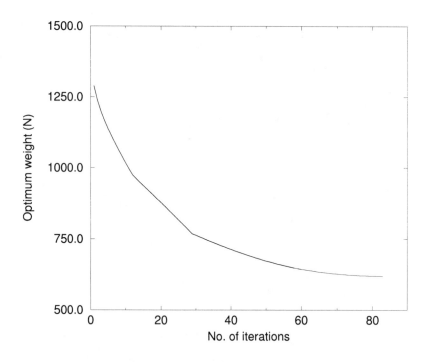

FIGURE 5.4 Convergence history for Example 1

0.645 cm^2 (0.1 in^2). Since there are three independent variables and 14 design constraints for each loading condition, the topology of the neural dynamics model consists of a variable layer with three nodes and two constraint layers with 14 nodes each (Figure 5.3).

Optimum design solutions from the neural dynamics model and previous research by Adeli and Kamal (1986) are given in Table 5.1. Figure 5.4 shows the convergence history for this example using a uniform structure as the starting point with all members having the same cross-sectional area of 6.45 cm^2 (1.0

Table 5.2 Allowable stresses for Example 2

Variable	Member	Compression MPa (ksi)	Tension MPa (ksi)
1	1	241.95 (35.092)	241.32 (35.0)
2	2, 3, 4, 5	79.91 (11.590)	241.32 (35.0)
3	6, 7, 8, 9	119.31 (17.305)	241.32 (35.0)
4	10, 11	241.95 (35.092)	241.32 (35.0)
5	12, 13	241.95 (35.092)	241.32 (35.0)
6	14, 15, 16, 17	46.60 (6.759)	241.32 (35.0)
7	18, 19, 20, 21	47.98 (6.959)	241.32 (35.0)
8	22, 23, 24, 25	76.41 (11.082)	241.32 (35.0)

in^2). An optimum weight of 617.9 N (138.91 lb) is found in this research. Adeli and Kamal (1986) reported 639.94 N (143.64 lb) for the same example. It is found that the active constraints at optimality are the x and y displacements of joint 1 for both loading conditions.

5.5.2 Example 2. 25-bar space truss

This example is a 25-bar space truss shown in Figure 5.5. The structure is symmetric about the X and Y axes. Thus, 25 members of the structure are linked to eight independent variables. The linked variables and the maximum allowable compressive and tensile stresses for the linked members are given in Table 5.2. The structure is subjected to the two load conditions given in Table 5.3. Displacement limits of $\pm$ 0.889 cm ($\pm$0.35 in) are imposed at joints 1 and 2 in the x and y directions. The lower bound of cross-sectional areas is given as 0.0645 cm^2 (0.01 in^2). Since there are eight independent variables and 29 design constraints for each loading condition, the topology of the neural dynamics model consists of a variable layer with eight nodes and

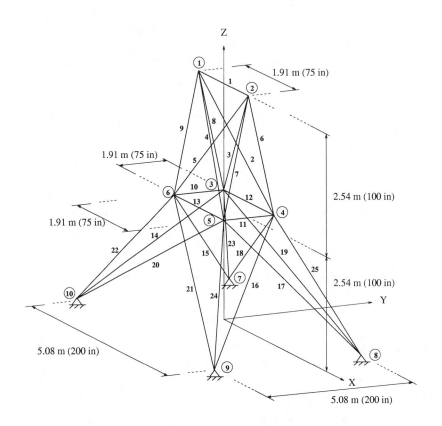

FIGURE 5.5 Twenty-five-bar space truss

Table 5.3 Loading conditions for Example 2

Loading condition	Loaded node	Load, kN ($kips$)		
		X	Y	Z
1	1	4.45 (1.0)	44.48 (10.0)	-22.24 (-5.0)
	2	0.0 (0.0)	44.48 (10.0)	-22.24 (-5.0)
	3	2.22 (0.5)	0.0 (0.0)	0.0 (0.0)
	6	2.22 (0.5)	0.0 (0.0)	0.0 (0.0)
2	1	0.0 (0.0)	88.96 (20.0)	-22.24 (-5.0)
	2	0.0 (0.0)	88.96 (20.0)	-22.24 (-5.0)

two constraint layers with 29 nodes. Optimum design solutions from the neural dynamics model and Adeli and Kamal (1986) are given in Table 5.4.

Table 5.4 Optimum solutions for Example 2

Variable	Member	Optimum solution, cm^2 (in^2)	
		Adeli and Kamal (1986)	Neural dynamics
1	1	0.0645 (0.0100)	3.0723 (0.4762)
2	2, 3, 4, 5	12.0897 (1.9855)	15.2096 (2.3575)
3	6, 7, 8, 9	19.1006 (2.9606)	16.6406 (2.5793)
4	10, 11	0.0645 (0.0100)	0.0645 (0.0100)
5	12, 13	0.0645 (0.0100)	0.0645 (0.0100)
6	14, 15, 16, 17	5.2013 (0.8062)	4.4090 (0.6834)
7	18, 19, 20, 21	10.8355 (1.6795)	10.3529 (1.6047)
8	22, 23, 24, 25	16.3213 (2.5298)	17.9593 (2.7837)
Optimum weight kN (lb)		2.427 (545.55)	2.453 (551.50)

Figure 5.6 shows the convergence history for this example using a uniform structure as the starting point with all members having the same cross-sectional area of 6.45 cm^2 (1.0 in^2). An optimum weight of 2.453 kN (551.50 lb) is found in this research.

Adeli and Kamal (1986) reported 2.426 kN (545.49 lb) and 2.427
kN (545.55 lb) for the same example, respectively. It is found
that the active constraints at optimality are the y displacement
of joint 1 and the compressive stress in member 9.

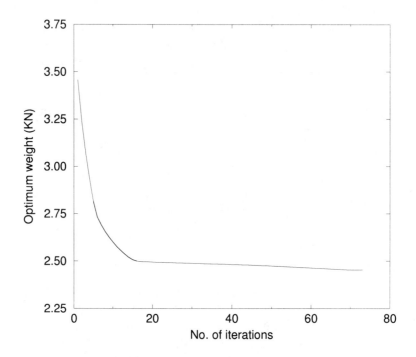

FIGURE 5.6 Convergence history for Example 2

5.5.3   Example 3. 72-bar space truss

This example is a 72-bar space truss shown in Figure 5.7.
The structure has two axes of symmetry in the horizontal plane.
The structure is subjected to the two loading conditions shown

Table 5.5 Loading conditions for Example 3

Loading condition	Loaded node	Load, kN ($kips$)		
		X	Y	Z
1	1	22.24 (5.0)	22.24 (5.0)	-22.24 (-5.0)
2	1	0.0 (0.0)	0.0 (0.0)	-22.24 (-5.0)
	2	0.0 (0.0)	0.0 (0.0)	-22.24 (-5.0)
	3	0.0 (0.0)	0.0 (0.0)	-22.24 (-5.0)
	4	0.0 (0.0)	0.0 (0.0)	-22.24 (-5.0)

in Table 5.5. Thus, 72 members of the structure are linked to sixteen independent variables, as identified in Table 5.6. The upper and lower bounds on the stress in each member are ± 172.4 MPa (± 25 ksi) in both tension and compression.

Displacement limits of ± 0.635 cm (±0.25 in) are imposed at the uppermost nodes in the x and y directions. The lower bound of cross-sectional areas is given as 0.0645 cm² (0.01 in²). Since there are sixteen independent variables and 80 design constraints for each loading condition, the topology of the neural dynamics model consists of a variable layer with sixteen nodes and two constraint layers with 80 nodes.

Optimum design solutions from the neural dynamics model and Adeli and Kamal (1986) are given in Table 5.6. Figure 5.8 shows the convergence history for this example using a uniform structure as the starting point with all members having the same cross-sectional area of 1.94 cm² (0.3 in²). An optimum weight of 1.675 kN (376.50 lb) is found in this research. Venkayya et al. (1969) and Adeli and Kamal (1986) reported 1.696 kN (381.20 lb) and 1.687 kN (379.31 lb) for the same example, respectively. It is found that the active constraints at optimality are the x and y displacements of joint 1.

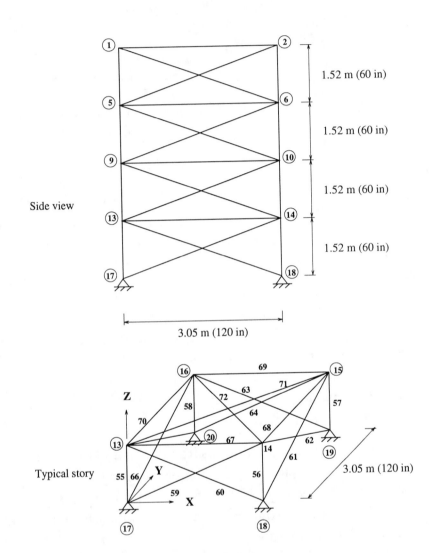

FIGURE 5.7 Seventy-two-bar space truss

Table 5.6 Optimum solutions for example 3

Variable	Member	Optimum solution, cm^2 (in^2)	
		Adeli and Kamal	Neural dynamics
1	1, 2, 3, 4	1.0187 (0.1579)	1.3875 (0.2151)
2	5, 6, 7, 8, 9, 10, 11, 12	3.5490 (0.5501)	3.3412 (0.5179)
3	13, 14, 15, 16	2.2252 (0.3449)	2.7029 (0.4190)
4	17, 18	3.2155 (0.4984)	3.2508 (0.5039)
5	19, 20, 21, 22	3.3142 (0.5137)	3.1012 (0.4807)
6	23, 24, 25, 26, 27, 28, 29, 30	3.0910 (0.4791)	3.2798 (0.5084)
7	31, 32, 33, 34	0.0645 (0.0100)	0.0645 (0.0100)
8	35, 36	0.0645 (0.0100)	0.4148 (0.0643)
9	37, 38, 39, 40	7.4626 (1.1567)	8.8361 (1.3696)
10	41, 42, 43, 44, 45, 46, 47, 48	3.6703 (0.5689)	3.2708 (0.5070)
11	49, 50, 51, 52	0.0645 (0.0100)	0.0645 (0.0100)
12	53, 54	0.0645 (0.0100)	0.0645 (0.0100)
13	55, 56, 57, 58	13.0703 (2.0259)	17.7722 (2.7547)
14	59, 60, 61, 62, 63, 64, 65, 66	3.4400 (0.5332)	3.2915 (0.5102)
15	67, 68, 69, 70	0.0645 (0.0100)	0.0645 (0.0100)
16	71, 72	0.0645 (0.0100)	0.0645 (0.0100)
Optimum weight, kN (lb)		1.687 (379.31)	1.675 (376.50)

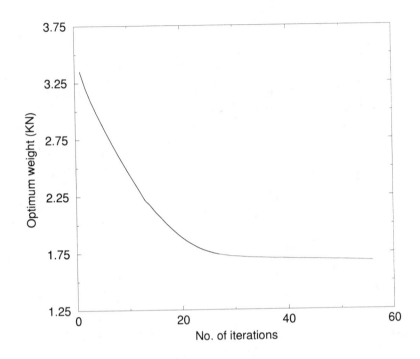

FIGURE 5.8 Convergence history for Example 3

5.5.4   Example 4. 1310-bar space truss

This example is a 1310-bar space truss shown in Figure 5.9. The 37-story space structure consisting of 332 nodes is symmetric about the X and Y axes. The 1310 members of the structure are divided into 146 groups as follows: In each story the vertical columns and horizontal members having the same length, and inclined members having the same length are grouped into the same categories. In the two tapered zones where the cross-section of the structure is reduced, inclined members having the same length are grouped into the same categories.

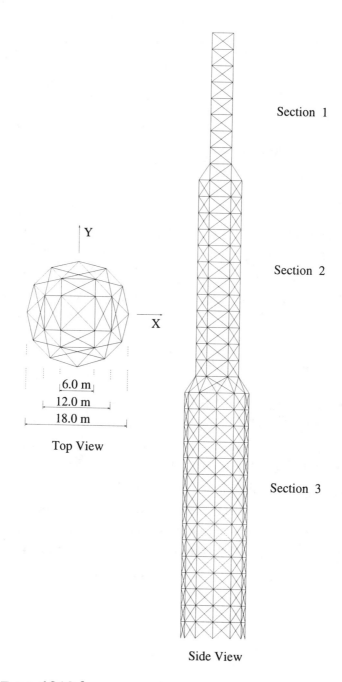

FIGURE 5.9 1310-bar space truss

The loading on the structure consists of vertical and horizontal loads. A uniform vertical load of 1.92 kPa (40.0 psf) is used at each floor. The lateral loads due to wind loads are assigned according to the Uniform Building Code (UBC, 1994). Lateral loads are determined by the normal force method, assuming the following values of coefficients for the wind load: the basic wind speed of 70 mph, exposure C, and an importance factor of 1. The upper and lower bounds on the stress in each member are ± 172.4 MPa (± 25 ksi) in both tension and compression. Displacement limits of ± 0.5 m (±19.69 in) corresponding to 0.4 % of the height of the structure of 129.5 m (424.9 ft) are imposed at the uppermost nodes in x and y directions. The lower and upper bounds of cross-sectional areas are given as 17.29 cm^2 (2.68 in^2) and 1387.09 cm^2 (215.0 in^2), respectively. Since there are 146 independent design variables and 1318 design constraints, the topology of the neural dynamics model consists of a variable layer with 146 nodes and a constraint layer with 1318 nodes. Figure 5.10 shows the convergence history for this example using a uniform structure as the starting point with all members having the same cross-sectional area of 300.0 cm^2 (46.5 in^2). An optimum weight of 2.515 MN (565410.24 lb) is obtained. This translates into 0.41 kPa (8.55 psf) when the total weight is divided by the total floor area provided by the structure. It is found that the active constraints at optimality are the y displacements of the four uppermost nodes (wind loads are applied in the y direction).

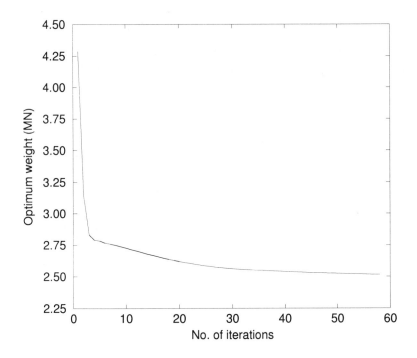

FIGURE 5.10 Convergence history for Example 4

5.6 Conclusions

A new computational method was developed for the optimization of structures using a nonlinear neural dynamics model. A pseudo-objective function was formulated for the optimization problem in the form of a Lyapunov function and its stability was proven mathematically. An appropriate neural network topology was presented consisting of one variable layer and a number of constraint layers equal to the number of loading conditions on the structure. The model was applied to the minimum weight design of four examples. It is concluded that the new approach results in a highly robust algorithm for optimization of large structures. Also, the new approach is amenable to parallel processing effectively.

Chapter 6

Hybrid CPN-Neural Dynamics Model for Discrete Optimization of Steel Structures

6.1 Introduction

There are two approaches to formulation of the constrained structural optimization problem. In the first and more common approach the design variables are assumed to be continuous (Adeli and Kamal, 1993; Adeli, 1994). In the practical design of steel structures, however, the designer usually must choose from a limited number of commercially available rolled shapes such as the widely used wide flange (W) shapes. Thus, in the second approach to structural optimization, design variables are treated as discrete variables. The number of articles published on the second approach is only a small fraction of the total articles written on structural optimization. Furthermore, discrete structural optimization articles are limited mostly to academic or small examples.

Liebman et al. (1981) used an integer gradient direction method for discrete minimum weight design of two-dimensional frame structures. Hua (1983) proposed implicit enumeration of eliminating the nonoptimal solutions and applied the concept to a minimum weight design of an 18-member aerospace wing box structure. Rajeev and Krishnamoorthy (1992) use a genetic algorithm for discrete optimization of structures and apply it to a 160-bar transmission tower. Cohn and Dinovitzer (1994) discuss why the application of structural optimization in practice is comparatively modest. In particular, they point out that the optimization trend among academic researchers is first to develop an algorithm and then seek problems for that algorithm rather than creating an algorithm for the solution of a given engineering problem.

Our goal is to develop novel and efficient algorithms for optimization of a given class of engineering problems, that is optimization of large steel structures consisting of a few thousand members selected among a few hundred commercially available sections. In Chapter 2, we presented application of counterpropagation neural (CPN) networks with competition and interpolation layers in structural analysis and design. In order to circumvent the arbitrary trial-and-error selection of the learning coefficients encountered in the counterpropagation algorithm, a simple formula was proposed as a function of the iteration number and excellent convergence was achieved.

In Chapter 4, a nonlinear neural dynamics model was presented for optimization of structures *assuming continuous variables* using the Lyapunov stability theorem. A learning rule was developed by integrating the Kuhn-Tucker necessary conditions for a local minimum with an exterior penalty function formulated as a Lyapunov functional. In this chapter, we present a hybrid counterpropagation-neural dynamics model for discrete optimization of structures and apply it to the minimum weight design of large steel structures.

6.2 Counterpropagation Neural Network

A CPN is a mapping neural network employing both Kohonen learning and Grossberg learning rules (Hecht-Nielsen, 1988). The topology of the CPN and the details of the training process were covered in Chapter 2.

Optimal design of steel structures according to commonly used design specifications such as the AISC Allowable Stress Design (ASD) specifications (AISC, 1989) requires computation of allowable member stresses. Allowable stresses in turn are functions of cross-sectional properties of the members. The allowable compressive stress of members in space axial-load structures is a function of the slenderness ratio, KL/r, where K is the effective length factor and r is the value of the radius of gyration of the cross-section. Assuming $K=1$, the allowable stress of a compression member is governed by r_y, the radius of gyration with respect to the minor axis of the cross-section. Thus, the efficiency of sections for carrying compressive forces generally increases as the ratio r_y/r_x approaches one (r_x is the radius of gyration with respect to the major axis). There are 295 W shapes in the AISC ASD manual (AISC, 1989). We are using a subset of this set as potentially economical sections for axial-force structures. This set consists of 61 W shapes for whom $0.5 < r_y/r_x < 1$.

The design variables in the structural optimization problem are cross-sectional areas of the members. But, the allowable compressive stress is a function of the radius of gyration of the cross-section. Thus, we need a strategy for mapping the two variables. In their continuous variable structural optimization formulation, Adeli and Balasubramanyam (1988) used a piecewise linear regression fit to approximate the relationship between the two variables. They show that it is not possible to represent this relationship accurately by a single curve or formula obtained from a regression analysis. Instead, they represented the relationship by a number of lines for each subgroup of W shapes such as W14 shapes.

In this work, we train a CPN network to learn the relationship between the cross-sectional area and the radius of gyration for the aforementioned subset of W shapes. The input is the cross-sectional areas of W shapes and the output is their radii of gyration about major (r_x) and minor (r_y) axes. The number of training instances is equal to the number of W shapes used (61). The result of training is stored in the form of 3X61=183 connection weights. The numbers of nodes in the competition and interpolation layers of the CPN network are 63 and 3, respectively.

Figure 6.1 shows the exact relationships between the cross-sectional area and the radii of gyration as well as those obtained from the trained CPN network. (Note that the values tabulated in the AISC manual are in inches. They have been transformed to the S.I. unit, cm.) Figure 6.1 demonstrates that the CPN network can represent the nonlinear relationships quite accurately. The error is in the order of 10^{-3} and therefore unnoticeable in Figure 6.1. As reported in Chapter 2, the required CPU time for training a CPN network is small and the network is easily expandable for adding additional W or other commercially available shapes. It took about 8 sec on an IBM RISC/6000 workstation to train the system for the relationships presented in Figure 6.1.

The relationship between the cross-sectional area and the radii of gyration is recalled in each iteration of the optimization

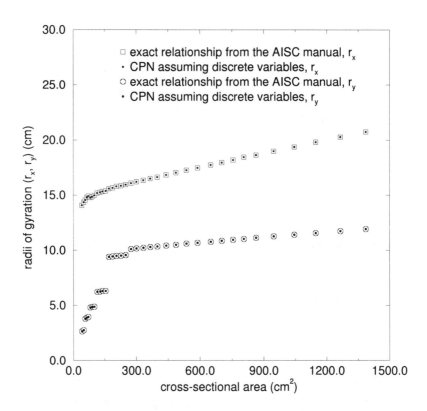

FIGURE 6.1 Relationship between the cross-sectional area and the radii of gyration

process using the trained CPN. This recalling process consists of two steps. The first step is to find the winning node among the nodes in the competition layer for a given input (Figure 6.2). When a continuous relationship is assumed between the input and output variables the number of winning nodes can be more than one (up to the number of nodes in the competition layer). In contrast, when input and output are discrete variables we set the number of winning nodes for each variable to one, and the value of the connection weight for the link connecting the winning node to the variable is close but greater than or equal to the value of the variable. Thus, a winning node is selected for each variable. After selecting the winning nodes for all the variables, the output (radii of gyration) is recalled in the second step based on the output from the winning nodes. The trained CPN maps an arbitrary given instance (design variable) to the nearest encoded output (radii of gyration).

6.3   A Hybrid Counterpropagation-Neural Dynamics Model for Structural Optimization

6.3.1   General

We present a hybrid counterpropagation-neural dynamics model and a new neural network topology for structural optimization of large structures with discrete members. The nonlinear neural dynamics model is based on Eq. (5.11) and acts as an optimizer to produce improved design solutions for given design constraints starting from some initial design solution and using first order sensitivity information. The sensitivity information and the magnitudes of the constrained violations, required for operations of the neural dynamics model, are evaluated based on the discrete cross-sectional properties. The discrete cross-sectional properties are provided by the trained CPN.

The hybrid neural dynamics model consists of four components: the neural dynamics model, counterpropagation neural network, structural analysis, and calculation of sensitivity coefficients. The information flow in the hybrid optimization model is presented schematically in Figure 6.2. The neural dynam-

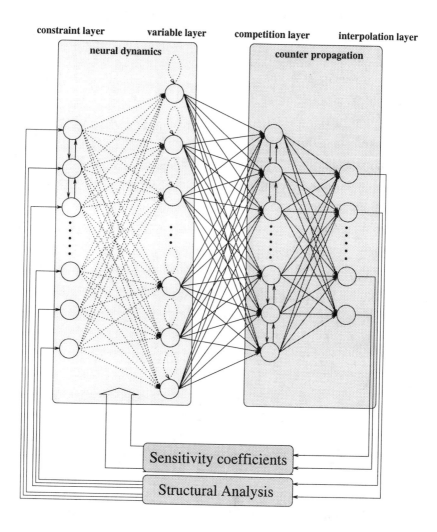

FIGURE 6.2 Information flow in the hybrid counterpropagation-neural dynamics model

ics model consists of two distinct layers: the variable layer and the constraint layer. Nodes in the constraint layer receive the discrete cross-sectional properties from the CPN as inputs, evaluate the prescribed constraints, and generate the magnitudes of constraint violations as outputs. The functional activations at the nodes in the variable layer receive information about the search direction (encoded as the weights of the links connecting the constraint layer to the variable layer) and magnitudes of constraint violations as inputs and generate the improved design solutions as outputs.

The number of stress constraints is equal to or a multiple of the number of members in the structure (for the case of multiple loadings). This number is in the thousands for a large structure with a few thousand members. As such, the number of violated stress constraints requiring computation of sensitivity coefficients tends to be very large. Thus, it requires an excessive amount of CPU time. We do employ a design variable linking strategy as is commonly done in the actual design of structures. The members grouped as one design variable have the same cross-sectional properties; but, each member in the group has a different magnitude of the constraint violation and different sensitivity coefficients for a given design solution.

To accelerate the optimization process and reduce the required CPU time for computation of sensitivity coefficients, only the most violated constraint in each group of members linked together as one design variable is allowed to represent the status of the stress constraint for that group. Therefore, a competition is introduced in the constraint layer to select the most critical node among the nodes belonging to one linked design variable. Let O_{ci} be the magnitude of constraint violation multiplied by the penalty parameter for the *ith* design variable (the output of a node in the constraint layer):

$$O_{ci} = r_n max\{0, max\{g_j(\mathbf{X})\}\} \qquad for \ j = 1, \ D_i \quad (6.1)$$

where D_i is the number of members grouped as the ith design variable.

The counterpropagation part of the model consists of two layers: competition layer and interpolation layer. Nodes in the competition layer receive the values of improved design solutions from the nodes in the variable layer, calculate the Euclidean distances between the input and the connection weights, and select the winning node. Nodes in the interpolation layer recall the corresponding cross-sectional properties encoded in the connection weights associated with the winning node.

The adjoint variable method (Arora and Haug, 1979) is used for sensitivity calculations. By using the adjoint variable method direct inverting of the structure stiffness matrix in the calculation of derivatives of displacements with respect to design variables is avoided. Sensitivity coefficients of the objective and constraints functions are also linked similarly to design variables (described in steps 2 and 10 of the hybrid algorithm to be presented in Section 6.3.3).

6.3.2   Topology

The topology of the hybrid counterpropagation-neural dynamics model is shown in Figure 6.3. The number of nodes in the variable layer is equal to the number of independent design variables (K) in the structural optimization problem. The number of nodes in the constraint layer is equal to the total number of constraints $(M + N)$ imposed on the structure.

The number of nodes in the competition layer (T) is equal to the number of available sections (in our case 61 for 61 W

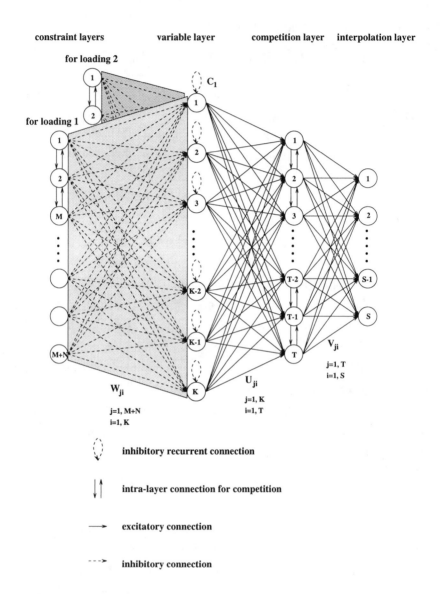

FIGURE 6.3 Topology of the hybrid counterpropagation-neural dynamics model

shapes). The number of nodes in the interpolation layer (S) is equal to the number of sectional properties required for calculation of the allowable stresses. This number is 3 for space axial-load structure $(A, r_x, \text{ and } r_y)$ and 11 for general space frame structures $(A, I_x, I_y, S_x, S_y, r_x, r_y, r_T, J, b_f, \text{ and } d/A_f)$.

Three types of connections are used to link nodes: interlayer connection, intra-layer connection, and recurrent connection. Nodes between different layers are connected by inter-layer links. In the neural dynamics parts of the model, sensitivity coefficients of constraints are encoded as weights of the inhibitory connections from the constraint layer to the variable layer $(W_{ji}, i = 1, K; j = 1, M+N)$. In the trained CPN part of the model, the cross-sectional areas of available W shapes are encoded in the connections from the variable layer to the competition layer $(U_{ji}, i = 1, T; j = 1, K)$ and their corresponding cross-sectional properties such as radii of gyration are encoded in the excitatory connections from the competition layer to the interpolation layer $(V_{ji}, i = 1, S; j = 1, T)$.

Intra-layer connections that link nodes in the same layer are employed to select the winning nodes in the constraint and competition layers. In the variable layer, the sensitivity coefficients of the objective function are assigned to the recurrent connections.

6.3.3 Hybrid algorithm

The hybrid counterpropagation-neural dynamics algorithm for structural optimization with discrete member sizes subject to displacement and stress (including buckling) constraints is presented in the following steps.

step 1. Initialize the design variables **X**, and select an initial value for the penalty parameter, r and the tolerance for the optimization convergence, ϵ.

step 2. Compute the linked sensitivity coefficients for the original objective function (weight of the structure).

$$C_i = \frac{\partial F(\mathbf{X})}{X_i} = \sum_{j=1}^{D_i} \frac{\partial F(\mathbf{X})}{\partial Y_j} \frac{\partial Y_j}{\partial X_i} \qquad i = 1,\ K \quad (6.2)$$

where X_i is the ith independent design variable, Y_j is the jth dependent variable in the ith design variable, and D_i is the number of dependent variables grouped as the ith design variable. Assign the coefficients to the inhibitory recurrent connections in the variable layer. Since we assume the geometry of the structure is fixed, the sensitivity coefficients of the objective function are constant during the optimization process. Thus, the inhibitory recurrent connection weights are assigned before the optimization iteration begins.

step 3. Set the iteration counter, $n=0$.

step 4. Feed forward the values of design solutions from the variable layer to the nodes in the competition layer of the CPN, and calculate the Euclidean distance between the ith design variable $(i = 1,\ K)$ and the connection weights U_{ij} between this variable and the T available standard shapes.

$$d_{ij} = \begin{cases} \| U_{ij} - X_i \| \ if & U_{ij} \geq X_i \\ & i = 1,\ K \ \ and \ \ j = 1,\ T \quad (6.3) \\ 0 & if \quad U_{ij} < X_i \end{cases}$$

step 5. Select the winning node among nodes in the competition layer for the *ith* design variable (i=1, K), and set the value of the output of the winning node (Z_{ij}) to 1.0 and remaining nodes to 0.

$$
Z_{ij} = \begin{cases} 1.0\ if & d_{ij} < d_{ik} \quad k = 1,\ T \\ & \qquad i = 1,\ K \quad and \quad j = 1,\ T \quad (6.4) \\ 0 & otherwise \end{cases}
$$

step 6. Recall discrete cross-sectional properties (for space axial-force structures, radii of gyration) based on the encoded weights of the links between the competition and interpolation layers connected to the winning node.

$$
A_i = \sum_{j=1}^{T} Z_{ij} V_{j1} \qquad i = 1,\ K \tag{6.5}
$$

$$
r_{xi} = \sum_{j=1}^{T} Z_{ij} V_{j2} \qquad i = 1,\ K \tag{6.6}
$$

$$
r_{yi} = \sum_{j=1}^{T} Z_{ij} V_{j3} \qquad i = 1,\ K \tag{6.7}
$$

step 7. Calculate the nodal displacements and member stresses by finite element analysis and find the allowable member stresses according to the AISC ASD (1989).

step 8. Calculate the outputs of nodes in the constraint layer using the following activation functions.

For stress constraint:

$$O_{cj} = r_n max\{0, g_j(\mathbf{X}^n)\} \qquad j = 1,\ M \qquad (6.8)$$

For displacement constraint:

$$O_{ck} = r_n max\{0, g_k(\mathbf{X}^n)\} \qquad k = 1,\ N \qquad (6.9)$$

Note that the commonly used sigmoidal activation function can not be used here because we are dealing with discrete variables. Also, a constant threshold (step) activation function cannot be used here because it transduces positive and negative activations (inputs) to 1 and 0 (outputs), respectively. By using Eqs. (6.8) and (6.9) instead, the output will be zero when constraints are satisfied and equal to the exact value of the violation when a constraint is violated.

step 9. Select the winning node in the constraint layer representing the most violated stress constraint among the members grouped as the *ith* design variable ($i = 1,\ K$).

$$O_{ci} = max\{O_{c1}, O_{c2}, \cdots, O_{cD_i}\} \qquad i = 1,\ K \qquad (6.10)$$

$$O_{cj} = 0 \quad if \quad j \neq i \qquad\qquad j = 1,\ D_i \qquad (6.11)$$

There is no competition among the nodes representing displacement constraints.

step 10. Calculate the sensitivity coefficients for the constraints associated with winning nodes (with nonzero output) and assign them as the weights of the inhibitory connections from the constraint layer to the variable layer.

$$w_{ji} = \frac{\partial g_j(\mathbf{X})}{\partial X_i} = \sum_{l=1}^{D_i} \frac{g_j(\mathbf{X})}{\partial Y_l} \frac{\partial Y_l}{\partial X_i}$$
$$i = 1, \ K \quad j = 1, \ M \qquad (6.12)$$

$$w_{ki} = \frac{\partial g_k(\mathbf{X})}{\partial X_i} = \sum_{l=1}^{D_i} \frac{g_k(\mathbf{X})}{\partial Y_l} \frac{\partial Y_l}{\partial X_i}$$
$$i = 1, \ K \quad k = 1, \ N \qquad (6.13)$$

step 11. Send the output from the nodes in the constraint layer $(O_{cj}$ and $O_{ck})$ to the nodes in the variable layer as their input. Calculate the input to the nodes in the variable layer as follows (based on Eq. 5.11):

$$\dot{X}_i = -C_i - \sum_{j=1}^{K} O_{cj} w_{ji} - \sum_{k=1}^{N} O_{ck} w_{ki} \quad i = 1, \ K \ (6.14)$$

step 12. Calculate the output for nodes in the variable layer using the activation function at the nth iteration given as $\int \dot{\mathbf{X}}(n-1)dt$

$$\mathbf{X}(n) = \mathbf{X}(n-1) + \int \dot{\mathbf{X}}(n-1)dt \qquad (6.15)$$

The improved values of design variables at the nth iteration, $\mathbf{X}(n)$, are calculated using the Euler method for numerical integration of the integral term in Eq. (6.15).

step 13. Check the optimization convergence or the change in the design variables by computing the following error function:

$$\Psi(n) = \sum_{i=1}^{K}\{X_i(n) - X_i(n-1)\}^2 \qquad (6.16)$$

If $\Psi(n) \leq \epsilon$ and outputs from the winning nodes in the constraint layer are all zero ($O_{ci}=0$ for all i=1, K), then $\mathbf{X}(n)$ is the solution. Calculate the value of the original objective function (the weight of the structure), and stop. Otherwise, increase the iteration counter, $n = n + 1$, update the penalty coefficient using

$$r_n = r_0\sqrt{n^3} \qquad (6.17)$$

and go to step 4. Based on numerical experimentations, we found Eq. (6.17) to produce stable and nonoscillating convergence.

6.4   Examples

We apply the hybrid counterpropagation-neural dynamics model presented in this chapter to minimum weight design of three example structures. The first example is taken from the literature for the sake of comparison. The remaining two examples are large steel structures created by the authors.

Table 6.1 Loading condition for Example 1

Loaded	Load, kN ($kips$)		
node	X	Y	Z
1	4.45 (1.0)	4.45 (1.0)	- 4.45 (1.0)
2	0.0 (0.0)	4.45 (1.0)	- 4.45 (1.0)
3	2.22 (0.5)	0.0 (0.0)	0.0 (0.0)
6	2.67 (0.6)	0.0 (0.0)	0.0 (0.0)

6.4.1 Example 1

This example is a 25-bar space truss shown in Figure 5.5. It is also solved by Zhu (1986) and Rajeev and Krishnamoorthy (1992). The modulus of elasticity and the specific weight for this example are E=68.95 GPa (10000 ksi) and ρ=27.14 kN/m³ (0.1 lb/in³), respectively. The information about loading conditions and groupings of members is given Tables 6.1 and 6.2. Displacement limits of ± 0.889 cm (±0.35 in) are imposed at joints 1 and 2 in X and Y directions. The maximum allowable compressive and tensile stresses are limited to ±275.6 MPa (±40 ksi). Twenty-five members of the structure are grouped into eight independent design variables. There are 4 displacement and 25 stress constraints. Thus, the numbers of nodes in the variable and constraint layers are 8 and 29, respectively.

The set of available sections consists of 30 discrete sections with cross-sectional areas given as { 0.1, 0.2, 0.3, 0.4, 0.5, 0.6, 0.7, 0.8, 0.9, 1.0, 1.1, 1.2, 1.3, 1.4, 1.5, 1.6, 1.7, 1.8, 1.9, 2.0, 2.1, 2.2, 2.3, 2.4, 2.5, 2.6, 2.8, 3.0, 3.2, 3.4 }(in²). Thus, each design variable can take any one of the 30 values during the optimization process. These 30 values are used for training the counterpropagation neural network. No buckling constraint is used in this example. Thus, the only required sectional property for this example is the cross-sectional area. As such, the numbers

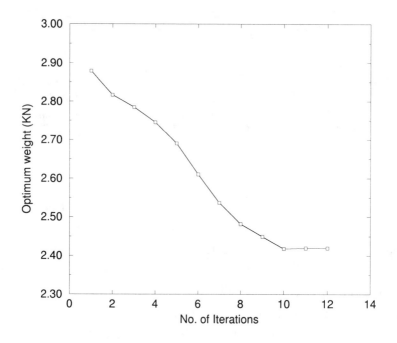

FIGURE 6.4 Convergence history for Example 1

of nodes in the competition and interpolation layers are 30 and 1, respectively.

The optimization convergence history is presented in Figure 6.4. A minimum weight of 2.420 kN (543.95 lbs) is obtained after 12 iterations. This compares with values of 2.429 kN (546.01 lbs) and 2.504 kN (562.93 lbs) reported by Rajeev and Krishnamoorthy (1992) and Zhu (1986), respectively.

6.4.2 Example 2

This example is a 1310-bar space structure modeling the exterior envelope of a 37-story steel high-rise building structure

Table 6.2 Optimum solutions for Example 1

Variable	Member	Optimum solution, cm^2 (in^2)		
		Zhu (1986)	Rajeev (1992)	Neural dynamics
1	1	0.65 (0.1)	0.65 (0.1)	3.87 (0.6)
2	2, 3, 4, 5	12.26 (1.9)	11.61 (1.8)	9.03 (1.4)
3	6, 7, 8, 9	16.77 (2.6)	14.84 (2.3)	18.06 (2.8)
4	10, 11	0.65 (0.1)	1.20 (0.2)	3.23 (0.5)
5	12, 13	0.65 (0.1)	0.65 (0.1)	3.87 (0.6)
6	14, 15, 16, 17	5.16 (0.8)	5.16 (0.8)	3.23 (0.5)
7	18, 19, 20, 21	13.55 (2.1)	11.61 (1.8)	9.68 (1.5)
8	22, 23, 24, 25	16.77 (2.6)	19.35 (3.0)	19.34 (3.0)
Weight, kN		2.504	2.429	2.420
(lb)		(562.93)	(546.01)	(543.95)

(Figure 5.9). The structure has 332 nodes and is doubly symmetric in the plan. It has an aspect ratio of 7.2. The 1310 members of the structure are divided into 105 groups. In the three main sections of the structure the same section is used for vertical members in every two stories, the same section is used for horizontal members with the same length in each floor. (There is only one type of horizontal member in sections 1 and 3; but, there are two different types of horizontal members in section 2.) The same section is used for inclined members in every story. In the two tapered transitional zones where the plan of the structure is reduced there are only inclined members that are grouped into one group in each tapered zone.

The basis of design is the AISC ASD specifications (AISC, 1989). Displacement limits of $\pm$ 0.5 m ($\pm$19.69 in) equal to 0.4 % of the height of the structure are imposed at the uppermost nodes in the X and Y directions. The modulus of elasticity of steel is E=198.91 GPa (29000 ksi) and the specific weight is

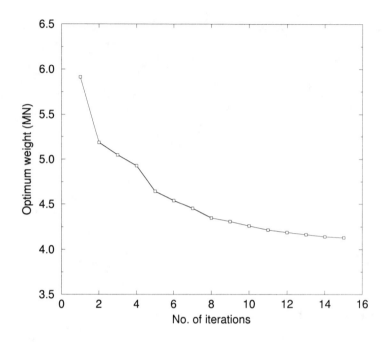

FIGURE 6.5 Convergence history for Example 2

ρ=76.97 kN/m^3 (490.0 lb/ft^3). Yield stress of F_y=344.75 MPa (50 ksi) is used.

The structure is subjected to two different loading conditions: dead plus live loads, and dead plus live plus wind loads. A uniform vertical load of 1.92 kPa (40.0 psf) is assigned to the nodes of each floor as vertical concentrated loads. The lateral loads due to wind are computed according to the Uniform Building Code (UBC) (1994). Lateral forces are determined by assuming a basic wind speed of 113 km/h (70 mph), exposure C (generally open area), and an importance factor of 1.

The lower and upper bounds for the selected set of 61 W

shapes are 24.71 cm^2 (3.83 in^2) and 1387.09 cm^2 (215.00 in^2). The required cross-sectional properties for this example are the cross-sectional area (A) and the radius of gyration (r_y). Therefore, the number of nodes in the competition and interpolation layers are 61 and 2, respectively. The convergence history for this example is shown in Figure 6.5. A minimum weight of 4.13 MN (928.64 kips) is found after 15 iterations. This translates into 0.68 kPa (14.84 psf) when the total weight of the structure is divided by the total floor area provided by the structure.

6.4.3 Example 3

This example is a large steel space structure modeling the exterior envelope of a 147-story superhigh-rise steel building structure (Figure 6.6). The structure has 1801 nodes and 8904 members and an aspect ratio of 7.2. It has three main sections: each section consists of 24 modules shown in Figures 6.7 and 6.8. Each module has 24 equal sides at each floor level and encompasses two stories of the structure.

The 8904 members of the structure are divided into 297 groups. Each module has four different types of members indicated in Figure 6.7. Member types 1 and 2 are horizontal members. Type 1 members connect adjacent nodes. Type 2 members connect alternate nodes. Member type 3 is slightly inclined from the vertical line (4 degrees in section 1, 3 degrees in section 2, and 2 degrees in section 3). Finally, the cross-bracing members are grouped as member type 4. In the truncated section 4, the grouping of the members is similar to sections 1 to 3. In the conical section 5 of the structure there are 24 members grouped as one type of member (Figure 6.8).

The basis of design for this example is also the AISC ASD specifications (AISC, 1989). Displacement limits of ± 1.98 m

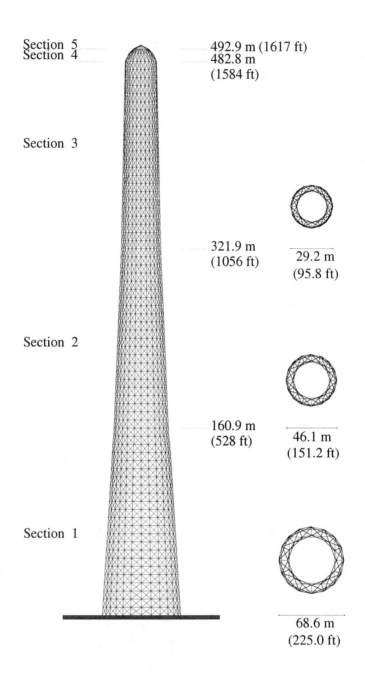

FIGURE 6.6 Example 3

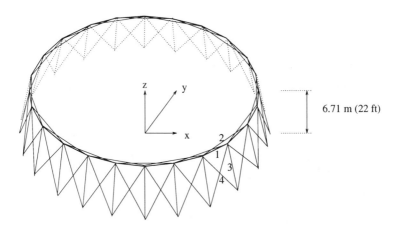

6.71 m (22 ft)

FIGURE 6.7 Details of the module for sections 1 to 3 of Example 3

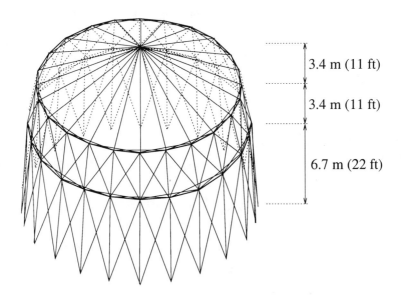

3.4 m (11 ft)

3.4 m (11 ft)

6.7 m (22 ft)

FIGURE 6.8 Details of the module for sections 4 to 5 of Example 3

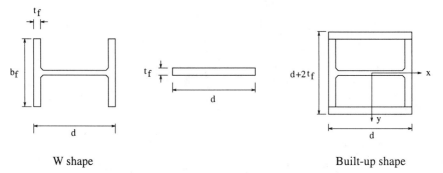

W shape   Built-up shape

FIGURE 6.9 Built-up shapes used in Example 3

($\pm$78.14 in) equal to 0.4% of the height of the structure are imposed at the uppermost nodes in the X and Y directions. Yield stress of F_y=344.75 MPa (50 ksi) is used. The structure is subjected to two different loading conditions similar to Example 2.

For this superhigh-rise structure, none of the W shapes commonly used for columns (with relatively high r_y/r_x ratio) were sufficient for the slightly inclined members in the lowest five modules. It should be noted that these members are quite long (22.10 ft = 6.72 m) in addition to being subjected to heavy axial forces. Therefore, we added additional built-up sections (BS) to our AISC sections database.

We created 14 box-type built-up sections by adding two plates to the ends of 14 W14 (14X223, 14X257, 14X283, 14X311, 14X342, 14X370, 14X398, 14X426, 14X455, 14X500, 14X550, 14X605, 14X665, and 14X730) shapes (Figure 6.9). For these sections, the thickness of the end plates is the same as the thickness of the flange plates rounded to the nearest 1/16 of an inch. The upper bound for the selected set of 61 W shapes and 14 built-up shapes is 2807.74 cm^2 (435.16 in^2). The lower bound is

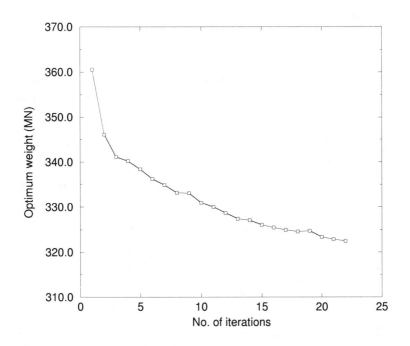

FIGURE 6.10 Convergence history for Example 3

the same as the previous example.

The required cross-sectional properties for this example are the cross-sectional area and the radius of gyration (r_y). The minor (y) axis for the built-up sections is noted in Figure 6.9. Therefore, the number of nodes in the competition and interpolation layers are 75 and 2, respectively. The convergence history for this example is shown in Figure 6.10. A minimum weight of 322.49 MN (72498.15 kips) is found after 22 iterations. This translates into 1.50 kPa (32.81 psf) when the total weight of the structure is divided by the total floor area provided by the structure.

6.5   Conclusions

A new hybrid counterpropagation-neural dynamics model was developed for structural optimization of large structures consisting of discrete sections and applied to minimum weight design of large steel structures subjected to multiple loading conditions and the constraints of the AISC ASD specifications. The discrete nature of design variables is incorporated in the optimization process by integration of an efficient counterpropagation neural network with little additional computational cost. In order to increase the efficiency of the algorithm the concept of using the most violated constraint in the optimization iteration is introduced by incorporating competition among the nodes in the constraint layer through the use of intra-layer links.

The computational model has been implemented in FOR-TRAN on the Cray YMP8/864 supercomputer. Three examples were presented, one small structure taken from the literature for the sake of comparison, and two large structures created by the authors. The convergence diagrams presented in Figures 6.4, 6.5, and 6.10 demonstrate the robustness of the algorithm. This is particularly significant for optimization of large steel structures subjected to the actual constraints of a commonly used design code.

Chapter 7

Data Parallel Neural Dynamics Model for Integrated Design of Large Steel Structures

7.1 Introduction

Concurrent processing on multiprocessor supercomputers (Adeli, 1992a & b) provides an opportunity to obtain optimization of large structures with thousands of members subjected to the highly nonlinear constraints of the actual design codes such as the American Institute of Steel Construction (AISC) Allowable Stress Design (ASD) or Load and Resistance Factor Design (LRFD) specifications (AISC, 1989 and 1994). In recent years the senior author and his associates have developed parallel algorithms for optimization and control of structures on shared-memory multiprocessors such as the Encore Multimax (Adeli and Kamal, 1993) and Cray YMP8/864 (Adeli and Cheng, 1994b; Soegiarso and Adeli, 1994 & 1995; Saleh and Adeli, 1994a & b, 1996, 1997; and Adeli and Saleh, 1998).

A high degree of parallelism can be exploited in neural computing models (Adeli and Hung, 1995). In this chapter, we present a robust data parallel neural dynamics model for discrete optimization of large structures on a massively parallel machine such as CM-5 and apply it to minimum weight integrated design of steel structures made of commercially available shapes. The integrated design consists of preliminary design, structural analysis, and the selection of the final members of the steel structure. As such, the final optimum solution is obtained automatically without any intervention from the user. Robustness of a structural optimization algorithm is of considerable significance since many structural optimization algorithms show convergence or instability problems when applied to large structures subjected to the actual highly nonlinear constraints of the AISC ASD or LRFD specifications.

In the following sections, we first briefly describe the nonlinear neural dynamics model for integrated optimum design of steel structures based on the AISC ASD or LRFD specifications. Next, we explain how the architecture of CM-5 is exploited in this research. Then, four data parallel structures and algorithms are presented for integrated design of steel structures. Next, the computational models are applied to minimum weight design of two large steel high-rise building structures ranging in height from 128.0 m (420 ft) to 527.0 m (1728.0 ft) and in size from 3228 to 20096 members. Finally, the chapter ends with a summary of performance results and conclusion. Performance of the data parallel neural dynamics model is presented in terms of speedup and million floating point operations per second (MFLOPS).

7.2   Nonlinear Neural Dynamics Model for Integrated Design of Steel Structures

We exploit parallelism in four stages of the neural dynamics optimization model:

- mapping the continuous design variables to commercially available discrete sections using a trained counterpropagation neural (CPN) network as explained in Chapter 6;

- generating the element stiffness matrices in the local coordinates, transforming them to the global coordinates, and solving the resulting linear simultaneous equations using the preconditioned conjugate gradient (PCG) method;

- evaluation of the constraints based on the AISC ASD or LRFD specifications; and

- computation of the improved design variables from the nonlinear neural dynamics model.

The four aforementioned stages of the model are described briefly in the following paragraphs.

The topology of the nonlinear neural dynamics model is shown in Figure 6.3. The design variables are the cross-sectional areas of the members. For integrated design of steel structures, a database of cross-sectional properties is needed for computation of element stiffness matrices and evaluation of the AISC ASD or LRFD constraints. For a general space frame structure, these properties include $S = 11$ entities (A, I_x, I_y, S_x, S_y, r_x, r_y, r_T, J, b_f, and d/A_f) for the ASD code and $S = 13$ entities (A, I_x, I_y, S_x, S_y, r_x, r_y, C_w, J, Z_x, Z_y, $b_f/2t_f$, and h/t_w) for the LRFD code. A counterpropagation network consisting of competition and interpolation layers is used to learn the relationship between the cross-sectional area of a standard wide-flange (W) shape and other properties such as its radii of gyration. In other words, the trained CPN network is used as the cross-sectional properties database manager. At every design iteration, the newly computed improved values of design variables are mapped concurrently to available W shapes and their corresponding cross-sectional properties.

The recalling process in the CPN network is done in two steps. In the first step, for each design variable a competition is created among the nodes in the competition layer for selection of the winning node. The weights of the links between the variable and the competition layers represent the set of cross-sectional areas of the available standard shapes. The weight of the link connecting the winning node to the variable is the one closest to the value of the variable itself but not smaller than that. In the second step, discrete cross-sectional properties encoded in the form of weights of links between the competition and the interpolation layers are recalled. The weights of the links connecting the winning node to the nodes in the interpolation layer are the cross-sectional properties corresponding to an improved design variable.

In the second stage of the nonlinear neural dynamics model for optimal design of steel structures, element stiffness matrices are first generated in the elements' local coordinates systems and then transformed to the global coordinates system. For solution of the resulting linear simultaneous equations, direct methods are not appropriate for distributed memory computers because of their large memory requirements. Direct methods require the assembly of the structure stiffness matrix which can be very large for a structure with thousands of members. Consequently, iterative methods such as the conjugate gradient method (Golub and Loan, 1989; Adeli and Kumar, 1995a & b) are deemed more appropriate for distributed memory computers where the size of local memory is limited, for example, to 8MB in the case of the CM-5 system used in this research. Computational efficiency of the conjugate gradient method can be improved by adopting pre-conditioning techniques (Van der Vorst and Dekker, 1988). As such, a data parallel preconditioned conjugate gradient (PCG) method is developed in this work.

The third stage consists of constraint evaluation using the nodal displacements and member stresses obtained in the previous stage. Three types of constraints are considered in this research: fabricational, displacement, and stress (including buckling). For the LRFD code, the primary stress constraint for a general beam-column member is a highly nonlinear and implicit function of design variables in the following form:

$$if \quad \frac{P_{uj}}{\phi_c P_{nj}} \geq 0.2$$

$$g_j(\mathbf{X}) = \frac{P_{uj}}{\phi_c P_{nj}} + \frac{8}{9}\left(\frac{M_{uxj}}{\phi_b M_{nxj}} + \frac{M_{uyj}}{\phi M_{nyj}}\right) - 1.0 \leq 0.0 \quad (7.1)$$

$$if \quad \frac{P_{uj}}{\phi_c P_{nj}} < 0.2$$

$$g_j(\mathbf{X}) = \frac{P_{uj}}{2\phi_c P_{nj}} + \left(\frac{M_{uxj}}{\phi_b M_{nxj}} + \frac{M_{uyj}}{\phi M_{nyj}}\right) - 1.0 \leq 0.0 \quad (7.2)$$

where P_{uj} is the required compressive strength of member j, P_{nj} is the nominal compressive strength of member j, M_{uj} is the required flexural strength of member j, M_{nj} is the nominal flexural strength of member j, and the resistance factors for compression and flexure are $\phi_c = 0.85$ and $\phi_b = 0.9$, respectively.

The nominal compressive and flexural strengths of a member are computed based on Chapters E and F of the AISC LRFD specifications (AISC, 1994), respectively. The required flexural strength of member j is computed by considering nonlinear second order effects (requiring additional structural analyses) as follows:

$$M_{uxj} = B_{1xj}M_{ntxj} + B_{2xj}M_{ltxj}$$

$$M_{uyj} = B_{1yj}M_{ntyj} + B_{2yj}M_{ltyj} \tag{7.3}$$

where M_{ntj} is the required flexural strength in member j assuming there is no lateral translation, M_{ltj} is the required flexural strength in member j due to lateral translation only, and B_{1j} and B_{2j} are magnification factors. Note that B_{1j} is evaluated for every beam-column and B_{2j} is evaluated for each story of a building structure.

For both AISC ASD and LRFD specifications, the effective length factor of a member, K, is computed by the equations presented in the European steel design code (Dumonteil, 1992). For braced frames:

$$K = \frac{3G_AG_B + 1.4(G_A + G_B) + 0.64}{3G_AG_B + 2.0(G_A + G_B) + 1.28} \tag{7.4}$$

and for unbraced frames:

$$K = \sqrt{\frac{1.6G_AG_B + 4.0(G_A + G_B) + 7.5}{G_A + G_B + 7.5}} \tag{7.5}$$

where the subscripts A and B refer to the joints at the two ends of the column under consideration. The factor G is defined as

$$G = \frac{\sum(I_c/L_c)}{\sum(I_g/L_g)} \tag{7.6}$$

in which I_c is the moment of inertia and L_c is the unsupported length of a column, I_g is the moment inertia and L_g is the unsupported length of a girder, and the summation ($\sum$) is over all the members connected to a joint and lying in the plane of buckling.

In the final stage, the nonlinear neural dynamics model acts as an optimizer to produce improved design variables from initial design variables. It consists of a variable layer and a number of constraint layers equal to the number of different loading conditions (Figure 6.3). The dynamic system describing how node activations change are described by (as noted in the previous chapter)

$$\dot{X}_i = -C_i - \sum_{j=1}^{M} O_{cj} w_{ji} - \sum_{k=1}^{N} O_{ck} w_{ki} \qquad i = 1, K \quad (7.7)$$

where X_i is the ith design variable (cross-sectional area of the group of members i), K is the number of design variables, M is the number of members in the structure, N is the number of constrained degrees of freedom, $\dot{X}_i$ is the time derivative of X_i and the input to the ith node in the variable layer, C_i is the inhibitory recurrent connection weight of the ith node in the variable layer, $O_{cj} = r_n max\{0, g_j(\mathbf{X}^n)\}$ is the output of the jth node in the constraint layer (representing a member stress constraint), $O_{ck} = r_n max\{0, g_k(\mathbf{X}^n)\}$ is the output of the kth node in the constraint layer (representing a nodal displacement constraint), w_{ji} ($i = 1, K$; $j = 1, M$) is the inhibitory connection weight from the jth node in the constraint layer (representing a member stress constraint) to the ith node in the variable layer, and w_{ki} ($i = 1, K$; $k = M + 1, M + N$) is the inhibitory connection weight from the kth node in the constraint layer (representing a nodal displacement constraint) to the ith node in the variable layer.

To derive the dynamic system represented by Eq. (7.7), the pseudo-objective function is formulated by transforming the constrained optimization problem into a corresponding unconstrained optimization problem using an exterior penalty function method. The resulting pseudo-objective function is in turn transformed to a Lyapunov function by verifying the stability of the pseudo-objective function. The dynamic system (Eq. 7.7) is derived by taking the derivative of the Lyapunov function with respect to time and making the value of the derivative less than or equal to zero. Therefore, the changes of node activations (the changes in the design variables) in the neural dynamics model are controlled such that the state of design variables approaches a desirable state (a local minimum) without increasing the value of the pseudo-objective function for the structural optimization problem. The changes in the values of design variables at the nth iteration are calculated by numerical integration of Eq. (7.7) using the Euler method. The improved values of design variables at the nth iteration are obtained as follows:

$$\mathbf{X}(n) = \mathbf{X}(n-1) + \int \dot{\mathbf{X}}(n-1)dt \qquad i = 1, \, K \qquad (7.8)$$

7.3   CM-5 Architecture

The main components of the CM-5 system (Figure 7.1) are a number of processing nodes (PN), partition managers (PM), and two high-speed, high-bandwidth communication networks called data and control networks (TMC, 1994a, b, c). A PN has four vector units (identified as VU0 to VU3 in Figure 7.1) with

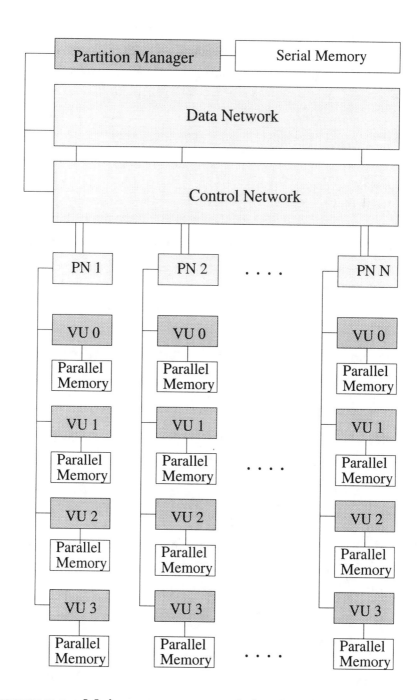

FIGURE 7.1 Main components of the CM-5

32 MB of total memory (8 MB per VU) and can perform high-speed vector arithmetic computations with a theoretical peak performance of 128 MFLOPS. A VU is the smallest computational element (processing element, PE) in the system which executes vector operations on data in its own local (parallel) memory. A 2^n ($n = 5, 6, 7, 8, 9$) number of PNs (32, 64, 128, 256, 512) is controlled by a partition manager. In the CM-5 system used in this work, a PM has 64 MB of serial memory and manages up to 2048 distributed PEs. Global communication operations involving all processors such as global summation or global synchronization are done via the control network. A data network is used for local communications (point-to-point exchange of data) between individual processing nodes.

Data on the CM-5 are divided into two classes: scalar (or serial) and parallel. Scalar data is stored in a PM memory and operated on serially by the PM. Operations involved in scalar or serial arrays must be minimized in order to achieve high parallel processing performance. Parallel data are distributed across parallel memories of VUs. The performance of a data parallel algorithm is highly dependent on the parallel data distribution method. Thus, parallel data must be distributed so that all PEs can work on data located in their own memory without any communication. In this research, we use a block distribution with detailed array layout to distribute parallel data. In block distribution, an array is divided into equal size blocks (the size of a block is specified in the array layout directive) and each block is assigned to one PE.

The programming language CM Fortran uses array processing features of Fortran 90 to express the data parallel algorithm. Array operations on a single array or array section (subset of an array) are processed concurrently on elements of the array allocated to the local VU memories. Array operations involving more than two arrays or array sections can be done efficiently without inter-processor communications only when corresponding elements of arrays are stored in the memory of the same VU (called conformable arrays). Two arrays are conformable when their dimensions and lengths are the same. For example, given two conformable one-dimensional arrays $X_1(2048)$ and $Y_1(2048)$ with 2048 elements, the multiplication operation $(X_1 * Y_1)$ can be done simultaneously in one step on 2048 VUs where each VU performs only one multiplication without any communication among VUs. Thus, for any given problem it is necessary to develop a data parallel algorithm and the corresponding data structures appropriate for the CM-5 data parallel architecture.

7.4 Data Parallel Structures and Algorithms

Four data parallel structures and algorithms have been developed for the problem of integrated optimal design of steel structures. The first one is for recalling the cross-sectional properties of the available standard shapes. The second one is for the PCG method used for the solution of the linear simultaneous equations. The third one is for evaluation of the AISC ASD or LRFD code constraints. The last one is for the operation of the neural dynamics network.

7.4.1 Recalling cross-sectional properties of the available standard shapes

For each design variable X_i (i=1, K) a competition is created to select the winning node in the competition layer. The

competition is processed by using the Euclidean distances between the *ith* design variable and the weights of the links connecting the *ith* design variable and the T nodes in the competition layers, U_{ij}, as follows (Figure 6.3):

$$d_{ij} = \| U_{ij} - X_i \| + \theta_{ij} \qquad for \quad j = 1, \ T \qquad (7.9)$$

where T is the number of available W shapes and θ_{ij} is set to
a large number greater than the maximum Euclidean distance
(for example, 10^5) if $U_{ij} < X_i$, otherwise $\theta_{ij} = 0$. This penalty
term, θ_{ij}, is adopted to select the winning node whose value
of the connection weight for the link connecting the *ith* design
variable is close but greater than or equal to the value of the
variable (to prevent the possible deterioration of the feasibility
of design solution at the given design iteration). Based on the
Euclidean distances, the winning node (Z_{ij}) is selected and the
output of the winning node is set to 1.0 and the remaining nodes
to 0:

$$Z_{ij} = \begin{cases} 1.0 \ if & d_{ij} < d_{ik} \qquad k = 1, \ T \\ & \qquad\qquad i = 1, \ K \quad and \quad j = 1, \ T \ (7.10) \\ 0 & otherwise \end{cases}$$

K competitions (the number of design variables) are required at each design iteration. To perform K competitions
concurrently, K design variables are divided into the same number of groups as the number of available PEs (N_p). Therefore,
each PE stores roughly $N_1 = K/N_p$ (rounded up to the next
integer) design variables and executes approximately the same
number of competitions concurrently. However, each competition involves computations of the Euclidean distances between
the value of a design variable and all the connection weights (U_{ij},
$j = 1, \ T$) because each design variable has the chance to be assigned a W shape and corresponding cross-sectional properties

from a given set of W shapes. In other words, the competition for a design variable requires inter-processor communications between the PE where the design variable is allocated and the PEs where cross-sectional properties of the set of W shapes are stored.

For any given X_i, the discrete sectional properties stored in the form of weights of links connecting the competition and interpolation layers, V_{jk} ($j = 1, T$; $k = 1, S$), are recalled based on the output of competition layer:

$$Y_{ik} = \sum_{j=1}^{T} Z_{ij} V_{jk} \qquad i = 1, K \quad and \quad k = 1, S \quad (7.11)$$

where Y_{ik} is the *kth* sectional property of the W shape corresponding to the *ith* design variable and S is the number of nodes in the interpolation layer (number of required sectional properties for each member). In this algorithm, to reduce the communication cost, private copies of U_{ij} and V_{jk} are broadcasted to each PE (Figure 7.2) which create a small initial overhead. In turn, each PE performs N_1 competition (Eqs. 7.9 and 7.10) and recalling (Eq. 7.11) processes concurrently without communications among PEs. With all the required data on the local memories of PEs the recalling process is operated concurrently without inter-processor communications. The data parallel recalling process is parallelized at design variable levels as follows:

step 1. Broadcast private copies of $\mathbf{U}(1 : T)$ and $\mathbf{V}(1 : T, 1 : S)$ to the PEs where the design variables are allocated.

(Each PE executes roughly N_1 operations concurrently in the remaining steps.)

step 2. Calculate the Euclidean distances, $\mathbf{d}(1:K, 1:T)$ between the design variables $\mathbf{X}(1:K)$ and the connection weights $\mathbf{U}(1:K, 1:T)$.

$$\mathbf{d}(1:K, 1:T) = \parallel \mathbf{U}(1:K, 1:T) - \mathbf{X}(1:K) \parallel \quad (7.12)$$

step 3. Set the values of $\theta(1, K, 1:T)$ and calculate the modified Euclidean distances, $\mathbf{d}(1:K, 1:T)$:

$$\begin{aligned}
&\textit{where} \quad \mathbf{U}(1:K, 1:T) - \mathbf{X}(1:K) < 0 \\
&\quad \theta(1:K, 1:T) = 10^5 \\
&\textit{else where} \\
&\quad \theta(1:K, 1:T) = 0 \qquad\qquad\qquad\qquad (7.13) \\
&\textit{end where}
\end{aligned}$$

$$\mathbf{d}(1:K, 1:T) = \mathbf{d}(1:K, 1:T) + \theta(1:K, 1:T)$$

step 4. Select the winning nodes based on the modified Euclidean distances, and set the outputs of the winning nodes, $Z(i=1:K, j=1:T)$ to 1.0 and remaining nodes to 0.

$$\begin{aligned}
&\mathbf{Z}\,(i = 1:K, j) \\
&= \begin{cases} 1.0\ \textit{if}\ \mathbf{d}(i=1:K, j) = \textit{min}\{\mathbf{d}(i=1:K, 1), \\ \qquad\qquad\qquad \cdots, \mathbf{d}(i=1:K, T)\} \quad (7.14) \\ 0 \qquad\qquad \textit{otherwise} \end{cases}
\end{aligned}$$

step 5. Recall discrete cross-sectional properties (S=11 for ASD and S=13 for LRFD) based on the encoded weights $\mathbf{V}(j = 1:T, k = 1, S)$:

$$\begin{aligned}
&\mathbf{Y}\,(i = 1:K, k = 1:S) \\
&= \sum_{j=1}^{T} \mathbf{Z}(i = 1:K, j)\mathbf{V}(j, k = 1:S) \qquad (7.15)
\end{aligned}$$

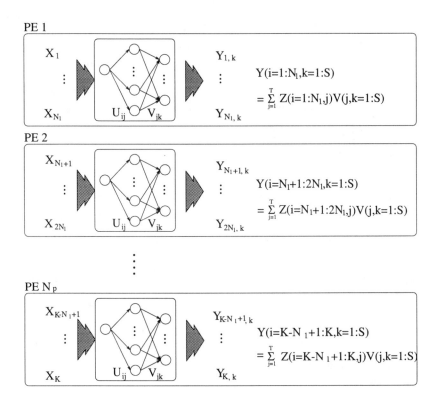

FIGURE 7.2 Distributed data structure for parallel re-calling process

7.4.2   Preconditioned conjugate gradient method

We present a data parallel PCG method with an appropriate data structure for the solution of linear equilibrium equations resulting from a finite element analysis of the structure. Two levels of parallelisms are exploited: structural elements level and degrees of freedom level. Each structural member and each degree of freedom is assigned to a VU explicitly.

For concurrent generation of element stiffness matrices, each element stiffness matrix containing $2N_2 X 2N_2$ components (N_2

= degrees of freedom per node) is assigned to a VU. These element stiffness matrices are stored uniformly across local memories of VUs in the form of unassembled global stiffness matrix
$\mathbf{K}(2N_2, 2N_2, M)$ (in the global coordinates) with the detailed
array layout $\mathbf{K}$(:serial,:sedrial,:block=N_m:procs=N_p) where
:serial directives lay out all the components of the specified dimensions of the array in the memory of a single PE, :block
directive specifies the number of components to be assigned to
each PE, and :procs directive specifies the number of PEs to
be used for the array. $N_m = M/N_p$ is the number of members
assigned to each PE. To overcome the problem of limited local
memory of a single PE, in our case 8MB per PE, element stiffness matrices are distributed on the memories of PEs without
explicit assembly of a global structure stiffness matrix. Furthermore, this data distribution mechanism ensures efficient load
balancing of PEs because each PE generates roughly an equal
number (N_m) of element stiffness matrices using sectional properties stored in its own local memory.

A diagonal preconditioner is set up from the diagonal elements of element stiffness matrices according to the nodal displacement connectivity matrix consisting of nodal displacement
indices of joints in members to accelerate the search process in
the conjugate gradient method. The diagonal preconditioner is
transformed into a vector whose length is the same as $N_2 X N_j$
(N_j = total number of joints in a structure). The major advantage of adopting the diagonal preconditioner is that its inverse
can be computed easily. All the data required in the process
of PCG are presented in the form of vectors with the same
length as the preconditioner except the element stiffness matrices that are defined as three-dimensional matrices. They consist of nodal load, displacement, error, and search direction vec-

tors. One degree of freedom is assigned to a VU. Consequently, $N_d = (N_2 X N_j)/N_p$ rounded up to the next integer is roughly the number of degrees of freedom assigned to each VU.

The major computations required for the PCG algorithm consist of basic linear algebra operations such as matrix-vector multiplications, dot products, scalar-vector multiplications, and vector additions. All vectors involved in the basic operations have the same data structure, a degree of freedom per VU. Thus, local vector updating operations are executed concurrently without inter-processor communication. However, communications are involved in both dot products and matrix-vector multiplications. Communication overhead involved in dot product operations, through the fast control network in the CM-5 system, is negligible compared to that of matrix-vector multiplications. A matrix-vector multiplication is required between the element stiffness matrix **K** and the search direction vector **p** for computation of the search step size.

Communication involved in the matrix-vector multiplications cannot be avoided on a distributed memory computer because the length and dimensions of the matrix and the vector are different. In our data parallel algorithm, the matrix **K** is distributed at the element level and the vector **p** is distributed at the nodal degree of freedom level. The matrix-vector multiplication is parallelized at the element level by transforming the direction vector **p** into an element level direction matrix in the form of a two-dimensional array **ptemp**$(2N_2, M)$ which is conformable with the unassembled global stiffness matrix **K**. This operation is performed by the sparse gather utility library function in the Connection Machine Scientific Software Library (CMSSL) (TMC, 1994b) using the nodal displacement connectivity matrix **IDJ**$(2N_2, M)$. As a result of the multiplication

we obtain the two-dimensional matrix **vtemp**$(2N_2, M)$ needed
for dot products in the remaining steps of the PCG algorithm.
Therefore, the two-dimensional array **vtemp** is transformed to
a vector $\mathbf{v}(N_d)$ by the sparse scatter utility in the CMSSL. The
sparse gather/scatter operations are performed in three steps:
set up the gather/scatter operation, perform the gather/scatter
operation, and deallocate the required storage space. Once routines for gather/scatter operations are set up, gather or scatter
operations can be called more than once without calling the
setup routines again. As such, communication cost is reduced
in the matrix-vector multiplication. The PCG algorithm parallelized at element and nodal degree of freedom levels is given as
follows:

step 1. Set up the diagonal preconditioner ($\mathbf{D}$) using the nodal
displacement connectivity matrix, and lay out elements
across the local memories of PEs by a degree of freedom
per PE.

step 2. Calculate the initial residual (error) vector ($\mathbf{r}_0$) and assign the search direction vector ($\mathbf{p}_0$), and compute the
temporary vector $\mathbf{z}_0$ and the scalar ρ_0 concurrently at the
node level using a starting vector ($\mathbf{u}_0$). *Each PE executes*
N_d/N_p *operations concurrently:*

$$
\begin{aligned}
\mathbf{r}_0(1 : N_d) &= \mathbf{P}(1 : N_d) \\
&\quad - \mathbf{K}(2N_2, 2N_2, M)\mathbf{u}_0(1 : N_d) & (7.16) \\
\mathbf{p}_0(1 : N_d) &= \mathbf{r}_0(1 : N_d), & (7.17) \\
\mathbf{z}_0(1 : N_d) &= \mathbf{D}^{-1}(1 : N_d)\mathbf{r}_0(1 : N_d), \quad and & (7.18) \\
\rho_0 &= \mathbf{z}_0^T(1 : N_d) \cdot \mathbf{r}_0(1 : N_d) & (7.19)
\end{aligned}
$$

step 3. Check the convergence of the PCG algorithm using the norm of the residual (error) vector, $\| \mathbf{r} \|$. If $\| \mathbf{r} \| \leq \varepsilon$, then $\mathbf{u}$ is the nodal displacement vector, and stop. Otherwise do the following steps.

step 3.1. Transform the direction vector into a temporary two-dimensional matrix using the gather operation via the nodal displacement connectivity matrix $\mathbf{IDJ}(2N_2, M)$.
gather [**ptemp, p**]

step 3.2. Do the concurrent matrix-matrix multiplications at element level. *Each PE executes N_m operations concurrently:*
$$\mathbf{vtemp}(2N_2, M) = \mathbf{K}(2N_2, 2N_2, M)\mathbf{ptemp}(2N_2, M)$$

step 3.3. Transform the matrix **ptemp** into the vector $\mathbf{v}$ using the scatter operation via the connectivity matrix $\mathbf{IDJ}(2N_2, M)$.
scatter [$\mathbf{v}(nd)$, $\mathbf{ptemp}(2N_2, M)$]

(Each PE executes roughly N_d/N_p operations concurrently in the remaining steps.)

step 3.4. Compute the step size for the search direction, $\gamma = \rho/\alpha$, where
$$\alpha = \mathbf{p}^T(N_d) \cdot \mathbf{v}(N_d)$$

step 3.5. Compute the improved nodal displacement vector.
$$\mathbf{u}(1 : N_d) = \mathbf{u}(1 : N_d) + \gamma \mathbf{p}(1 : N_d)$$

step 3.6. Calculate new residual vector.
$$\mathbf{r}(1 : N_d) = \mathbf{r}(1 : N_d) + \gamma \mathbf{p}(1 : N_d)$$

step 3.7. Compute new search direction vector and go to step 3.

$$\mathbf{p}(1:N_d)=\mathbf{z}(1:N_d)+\beta\mathbf{p}(1:N_d)$$
$$\mathbf{z}(1:N_d)=\mathbf{M}^{-1}(1:N_d)\mathbf{r}(1:N_d)$$
$$\rho_i=\mathbf{z}(N_d)_0^T\cdot\mathbf{r}(N_d)]$$
$$\beta=\rho_i/\rho_{i-1}$$

7.4.3   Constraint evaluation

Three different kinds of constraints are considered in the formulation of structural optimization problems: fabrication, displacement, and stress constraints. Displacement constraints can be evaluated directly using the nodal displacement vector from the PCG solver. Stress constraints are based on the AISC ASD (AISC, 1989) or LRFD (AISC, 1994) specifications.

Constraints evaluation requires cross-sectional properties of W shapes used for members in a structure. They are obtained from the trained CPN network as described previously. The cross-sectional properties are distributed element-wise such that all cross-sectional properties for a member reside in the memory of a single VU. N_m allowable member stresses for ASD code or nominal member strengths for the LRFD code are computed on each single VU. Thus, the computations related to constraints evaluation are processed concurrently at the element level.

7.4.4   Operation of the neural dynamics network

In a neural network model, the input to a node is calculated by the weighted sum of outputs from the nodes in the previous layer. In our model, the input to the ith node in the variable layer is the sum of three terms (Eq. 7.7): the inhibitory recurrent connection weight of the ith node in the variable layer, C_i; the weighted sum of outputs from the nodes representing nodal displacement constraints in the constraint layer, $\sum_{j=1}^M O_{cj}w_{ji}$;

and the weighted sum of outputs from the nodes representing member stress constraints in the constraint layer, $\sum_{k=1}^{N} O_{ck} w_{ki}$.

In the dynamic system, the computation of the inputs to the nodes in the variable layer (Eq. 7.7) are parallelized at both node and weight levels. For node level parallelism, a node in each layer is assigned to a PE. In turn, each PE computes roughly $N_3 = M + N/N_p$ and N_1 rounded up to the next integer outputs of the nodes in the constraint and variable layers, respectively. They are operated concurrently without any inter-processor communication.

For the computations of inputs to the nodes in the variable layer, each column of the matrix representing the connection weights, $w_{ji}(j = 1 : M + N, i = i_1)$, between the i_1 node in the variable layer and all the nodes in the constraint layer $(j = 1, M + N)$ is mapped to a VU. Each PE stores roughly N_1 columns of the weight matrix. The connection weights, $C_i(i = 1 : K)$, are distributed the same as the nodes in the variable layer. However, it requires inter-processor communications because each column of the matrix requires the vector of outputs from nodes in the constraint layer for the multiplication. In this algorithm, to reduce the communication cost, private copies of O_{cj} and O_{ck} are broadcasted to PEs where the columns of the connection weight matrix reside.

With N_1 columns of the connection weight matrix and the private copy of the output vector from the nodes in the constraint layer, the computations of inputs to the nodes in the variable layer are parallelized at both the node (neuron) and weight levels as follows:

step 1. Broadcast private copies of O_{cj} and O_{ck} to the PEs where the columns of the connection weight matrix are allocated.

(Each PE executes roughly N_1 operations concurrently in the remaining steps.)

step 2. Calculate the weighted sum of outputs from the nodes in the constraint layer

$$\dot{\mathbf{X}}(1:K) = -\sum_{j=1}^{M} \mathbf{O}_c(j)\mathbf{w}(j, 1:K)$$
$$-\sum_{k=1}^{N} \mathbf{O}_c(k)\mathbf{w}(k, 1:K) \qquad (7.20)$$

step 3. Calculate the inputs to the nodes in the variable layer

$$\dot{\mathbf{X}}(1:K) = \dot{\mathbf{X}}(1:K) - \mathbf{C}(1:K) \qquad (7.21)$$

step 4. Calculate the outputs of the nodes in the variable layer (improved values of the design variables) by the numerical integration.

$$\mathbf{X}(1:K) = \mathbf{X}(1:K) + \int \dot{\mathbf{X}}(1:K) \qquad (7.22)$$

7.5 Examples

The data parallel structural optimization neural dynamics model presented in this chapter has been implemented on the CM-5 (TMC, 1994a) using CM Fortran (TMC, 1994b) (Figure 7.3). The model is applied to minimum weight design of two large steel space moment resisting frames with cross bracings.

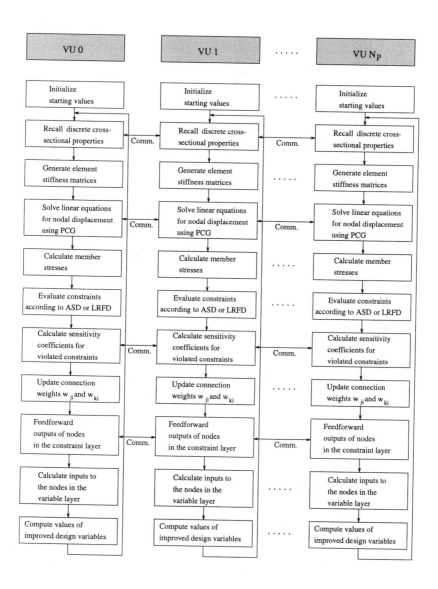

Comm. : communication is required

FIGURE 7.3 Data parallel structural optimization algorithm

The modulus of elasticity of steel is E=198.91 GPa (29000 ksi) and the specific weight is ρ=76.97 kN/m^3 (490 lb/ft^3). Yield stress of F_y=344.75 MPa (50 ksi) is used for all examples.

7.5.1 Example 1

This example is a 36-story irregular steel moment-resisting space frame with setbacks and cross bracings (Figures 7.4 and 7.5). The structure has 1384 nodes and an aspect ratio of 4.7. The 3228 members of the structure are divided into 186 groups. The structure is divided into three 12-story sections as indicated in Figure 7.5. In sections 1 and 2 of the structure four different types of columns are used in every two stories as follows: corner columns, outer columns, inner columns in unbraced frames, and inner columns in braced frames. In section 3, there are only the first three different types of columns. In sections 1 and 2, the beams of each story are divided into 3 groups: outer beams, inner beams in braced frames, and inner beams in unbraced frames. In section 3, there are only the first two types of beams. Two different types of bracings are used in every three stories: one type in the longitudinal and another type in the transverse direction.

For displacement constraints, the interstory drift is limited to 0.004 times the story height in x and y directions (Figure 7.5). The loading on the structure consists of dead load of 2.88 kPa 60(psf), live load 2.38 kPa of (50psf), and roof live load of 2.38 kPa(50psf). The lateral loads due to wind are computed according to the Uniform Building Code (UBC) (1994). Lateral forces are determined by assuming a basic wind speed of 113 km/h (70 mph), exposure C (generally open area), and an importance factor of 1.

There are 295 W shapes in the AISC LRFD manual. Not all

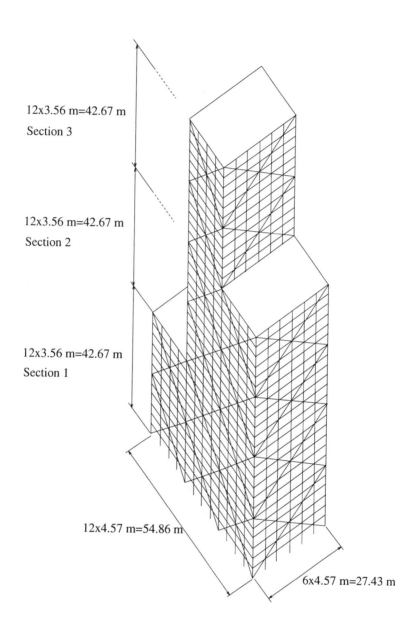

12x3.56 m=42.67 m
Section 3

12x3.56 m=42.67 m
Section 2

12x3.56 m=42.67 m
Section 1

12x4.57 m=54.86 m

6x4.57 m=27.43 m

FIGURE 7.4 Example 1

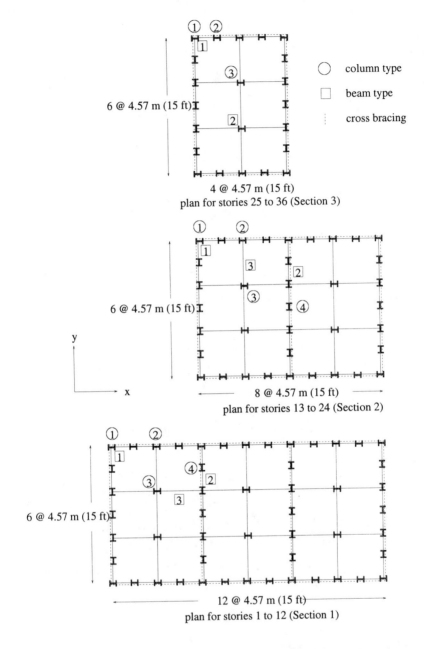

4 @ 4.57 m (15 ft)
plan for stories 25 to 36 (Section 3)

6 @ 4.57 m (15 ft)

column type
beam type
cross bracing

y

x

8 @ 4.57 m (15 ft)
plan for stories 13 to 24 (Section 2)

6 @ 4.57 m (15 ft)

12 @ 4.57 m (15 ft)
plan for stories 1 to 12 (Section 1)

6 @ 4.57 m (15 ft)

FIGURE 7.5 Floor plan for Example 1

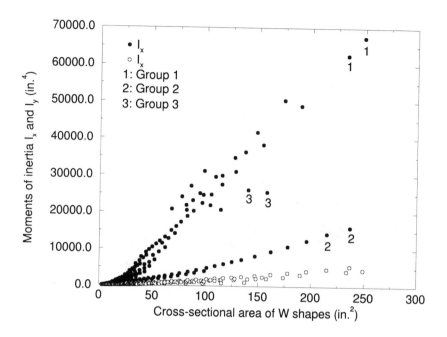

FIGURE 7.6 Relationship between the cross-sectional area and the moments of inertia I_x and I_y for the 295 W shapes available in the AISC LRFD manual

are considered economical shapes as beam and column members used in high-rise building structures. Broadly speaking, suitable W shapes for beam members are those with a large moment of inertia I_x, and suitable W shapes for columns are those with radii of gyrations r_x and r_y close to each other. Figure 7.6 shows the relationships between the moments of inertia I_x and I_y and the cross-sectional area of the 295 W shapes available in the AISC LRFD manual (AISC, 1994). Figure 7.7 shows similar relationships between the radii of gyrations r_x and r_y and the cross-sectional area.

Three trends are observed in Figures 7.6 and 7.7. For one

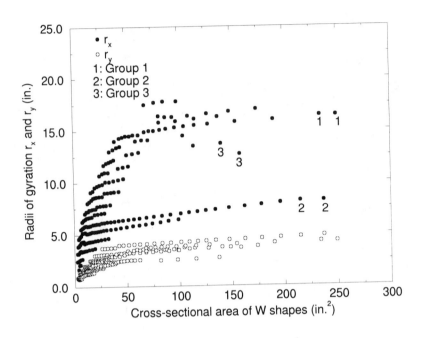

FIGURE 7.7 Relationship between the cross-sectional area and the radii of gyration r_x and r_y for the 295 W shapes available in the AISC LRFD manual

group of W shapes (identified by 1 in Figures 7.6 and 7.7) the moment of inertia with respect to the major axis, I_x (or radius of gyration, r_x), is substantially larger than the moment of inertia with respect to the minor axis, I_y (or radius of gyration, r_y). These W shapes are suitable as beam members. For the second group of W shapes (identified as 2 in Figures 7.6 and 7.7), I_x and I_y values are relatively close to each other. The third group of W shapes falls in between (identified by 3 in Figures 7.6 and 7.7).

We have deleted the third group of W shapes and those with cross-sectional areas less than 32.3 cm^2 (5 in^2) from our sections

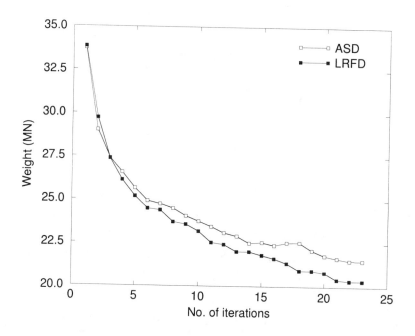

FIGURE 7.8 Convergence history for Example 1

database altogether. We have chosen 162 W shapes from the first group as potentially economical beam sections and 58 W shapes from the second group as potentially economical column sections.

The lower bounds for column/bracing and beam members are 35.7 cm² (5.54 in²) and 33.9 cm² (5.26 in²), respectively. The upper bounds for column/bracing and beam members are 1529.0 cm² (237.0 in²) and 1606.4 cm² (249.0 in²), respectively.

The convergence histories for designs AISC ASD and LRFD codes are shown in Figure 7.8. Minimum weights of 21.51 MN (4836.6 kips) and 20.34 MN (4573.5 kips) are obtained using the ASD and LRFD codes, respectively. These translate into 0.59

kPa (12.44 psf) and 0.56 kPa (11.76 psf) for ASD and LRFD codes, respectively, when the total weight of the structure is divided by the total floor area provided by the structure. The minimum weight design based on the LRFD code is 5.4 % lighter than that based on the ASD code.

7.5.2   Example 2

This example is a 144-story steel superhigh-rise building structure with a height of 526.7 m (1728 ft) (Figure 7.9). The structure is a modified tube-in-tube system consisting of a space moment-resisting frame with cross bracings on the exterior of the structure. The structure has 8463 nodes and an aspect ratio of 7.2. The 20096 members of the structure are divided into 568 groups (Figure 7.10). In section 1 of the structure, five different types of columns are used in every two stories as follows: corner columns in the outer tube, non-corner columns in the outer tube, columns in the middle tube, columns in the inner tube, and the center column. Four different types of beams are used in every two stories as follows: beams in the outer tube, beams in the middle tube, beams in the inner tube, and beams connecting and within the tubes. Two types of bracings cover every six stories: one type covers the faces AB, CD, DE, and AF and the other type covers the two corner regions BC and EF (Figure 7.10).

In section 2, four different types of columns are used in every two stories as follows: corner columns in the outer tube, non-corner columns in the outer tube, columns in the inner tube, and the center column. The beams of every two stories are divided into three groups: beams in the outer tube, beams in the inner tube, and beams connecting and within the tubes. The same type of bracings is used in every six stories.

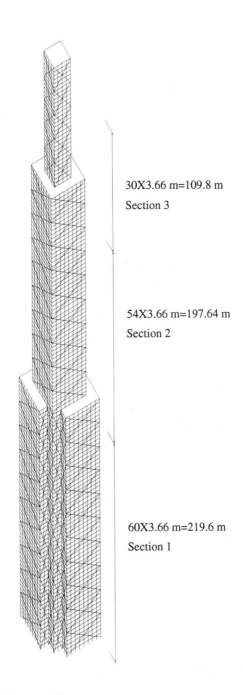

30X3.66 m=109.8 m

Section 3

54X3.66 m=197.64 m

Section 2

60X3.66 m=219.6 m

Section 1

FIGURE 7.9 Example 2

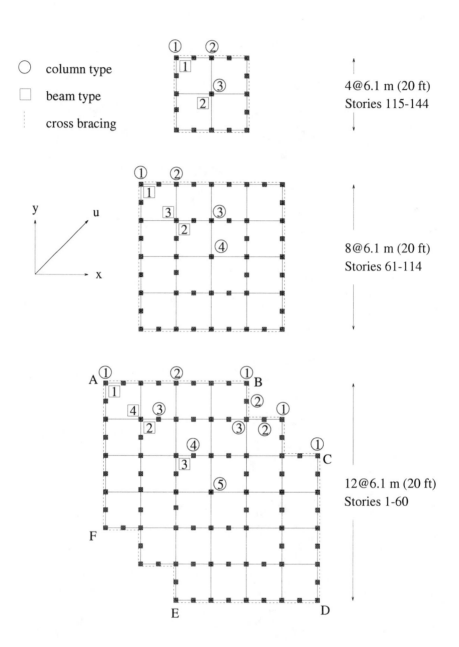

FIGURE 7.10 Floor plan for Example 2

In section 3, three different types of columns are used in every two stories as follows: corner columns, outer columns, and a center column. The beams of every two stories in this section are divided into two groups: inner beams and outer beams. The same type of bracings is used in every six stories.

For displacement constraints, the interstory drift is limited to 0.004 times the story height in both x and y directions. The loading on the structure consists of a dead load of 2.40 kPa (50 psf), live load 2.40 kPa (50 psf) in section 1 and dead load of 2.40 kPa (50 psf), live load 1.92 kPa (40 psf), and roof live load 1.92 kPa (40 psf) in sections 2 and 3. The structure is subjected to wind loads based on the UBC code similar to Example 1. In this example, wind loads are applied in three different directions x, y, and u (Figure 7.10).

The lower bounds for column/bracing and beam members are 35.7 cm^2 (5.54 in^2) and 33.9 cm^2 (5.26 in^2), respectively. The upper bounds for column/bracing and beam sections are 2807.74 cm^2 (435.16 in^2) and 1606.4 cm^2 (249.0 in^2), respectively.

The convergence histories for designs based on AISC ASD and LRFD codes are shown in Figure 7.11. Minimum weights of 682.2 MN (153381.4 kips) and 669.3 MN (150467.2 kips) are obtained using the ASD and LRFD codes, respectively. These translate into 1.57 kPa (34.43 psf) and 1.54 kPa (33.78 psf) for ASD and LRFD codes, respectively. The minimum weight design based on the LRFD code is about 2.0% lighter than that based on the ASD code. It may be noted that the amount of steel used in the currently tallest steel building structure in world, the 109-story Sears building in Chicago with a height of 445.0 m, is 33 psf (Adeli, 1988).

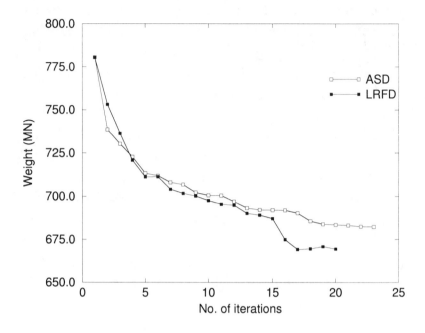

FIGURE 7.11 Convergence history for Example 2

7.6   Performance Results and Conclusions

Performance of a data parallel algorithm can be enhanced by creating appropriate data structures for a particular problem, maximizing the parallel computations, and minimizing the interprocessor communication. In this chapter, we presented a data parallel neural dynamics computing model for integrated optimum design of large steel structures consisting of thousands of members and subjected to the constraints of two commonly used design codes. The model was implemented in CM Fortran on a CM-5 supercomputer.

To achieve high performance, all the data are processed as parallel arrays across the VUs such that the elements that need to be operated together reside in the local parallel memory of the same VU. To do this, the elements in each parallel array to be assigned to a VU are explicitly specified by detailed array layout directives without any dependency on the machine configuration.

Efficient load balancing is ensured by distributing the array elements among the available VUs evenly. On a distributed memory architecture such as the CM-5 supercomputer, the small size of the local memory of each VU is a major obstacle in handling large structures with thousands of members. To overcome this problem, a bi-level data parallel element-by-element PCG algorithm was developed for the solution of the resulting simultaneous linear system of equations. In this algorithm, each member stiffness matrix and each degree of freedom are assigned to a VU.

To maximize the efficiency of parallel computations, all the parallel arrays are made conformable even though the ranks and dimensions of arrays are different. This is done by selecting subsets of the elements of arrays to be conformable array sections. Performance rates of parallel computations for the 256-node configuration are summarized in Table 7.1. Timing results presented in this table as well as in Tables 7.2 and 7.3 are in terms of the CM busy time (TMC, 1994a). The CM busy time is the time spent in executing parallel computations on the selected number of PNs. For double precision operations used for Example 2, a peak parallel computation performance of approximately 3.69 GFLOPS was obtained at the 256-node configuration.

Parallel communications involving data exchange among processors are handled by two internal communication networks:

Table 7.1 Performance rates of parallel computations for the 256-node configuration (10^6 floating point operations/10^{-3} sec = GFLOPS)

	Precision	Stiffness matrix generation	PCG iterations	Operations of neural dynamics
Example 1	double	0.38/0.16 = 2.38	1.04/1.53 = 0.68	0.086/0.37 = 0.23
Example 2	double	33.30/9.02 = 3.69	6.45/4.10 = 1.57	0.686/0.46 = 1.49

Table 7.2 CM busy time for the initial broadcasting and the recalling process using a 256-node configuration (in milliseconds)

	Broadcasting	Recalling
Example 1	2.31	13.80
Example 2	2.40	37.52

control network and data network. Communication overhead involved in the global reduction operations such as dot product computation between vectors distributed across processors is unavoidable. But, this overhead is small in our model.

For the communication intensive parts of the model such as the recalling process and the operation of the neural dynamic system, interprocessor communications are reduced by broadcasting multiple copies of data to the target processor and paying only a small initial communication cost. The CM busy times for the initial broadcasting and the recalling process for the two examples are given in Table 7.2. This table shows that the ratio of broadcasting time to the time required in the recalling process is about 6.4% for the space frame example structures 1 and 2 which is small.

For the operations of the neural dynamic system, we ex-

Table 7.3 The average number of iterations and CM busy time for the PCG solver using a 256-node configuration

	Number of degrees of freedom	Number of iterations	CM busy time in seconds
Example 1	8304	524	3.56
Example 2	50778	1850	24.38

Table 7.4 The overall wall-clock time for complete optimum design using a 256-node configuration (in minutes)

	ASD	LRFD
Example 1	13.1	30.1
Example 2	117.0	196.5

ploited parallelism at two levels: node (neuron) level and link weight level. This, plus the all-to-all broadcasting used in the operation of the neural dynamic system, resulted in a reduction of the CM busy time from 0.045 sec to 0.016 sec for Example 2 using a 256-node configuration.

The overall CM busy time for one complete iteration of the optimization process depends heavily on the execution time of the PCG solver. The PCG solver routine calls for both structural analysis and sensitivity analysis. The number of iterations required in the PCG algorithm increases with the number of degrees of freedom of the structure. The average number of PCG iterations and the CM busy times for the two example structures using 256-node configuration are summarized in Table 7.3.

The overall wall-clock times for complete integrated optimum design of two example structures using a 256-node configuration are presented in Table 7.4. Finally, Figure 7.12 presents the speedup curves for the two examples for the 64-, 128-, and

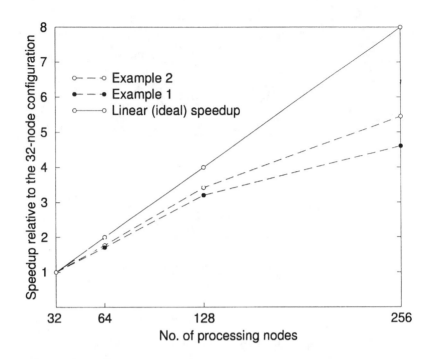

FIGURE 7.12 Relative speedup curves for the two examples

256-node configurations relative to the 32-node configuration. It is observed that the speed up increases with an increase in the size of the structure.

To summarize, we presented a robust data parallel computational model for discrete optimization of large structures and applied it to integrated minimum weight design of steel structures. The convergence histories in Figures 7.8 and 7.11 demonstrate the robustness and stability of the computational model. In fact, we noted the model is insensitive to the selection of the initial design. This is specially noteworthy because we applied the model to optimization of large space frame structures subjected to actual design constraints of the AISC ASD and LRFD specifications. In particular, the constraints of the LRFD code are complicated and highly nonlinear and implicit functions of design variables. Further, the LRFD code requires the consideration of the nonlinear second order $P\delta$ and $P\Delta$ effects (AISC, 1994).

Chapter 8

Distributed Neural Dynamics Algorithms for Optimization of Large Steel Structures

8.1 Introduction

High-performance multiprocessors are broadly classified into shared memory and distributed memory machines. In a shared memory machine, a few powerful processors are connected to a single shared memory. Each processor can access any part of the shared memory. This makes implementation relatively simple, but the resulting memory contention creates a bottleneck when several processors try to access the same memory location. In a distributed memory machine, on the other hand, a relatively large number of microprocessors are connected to their own locally distributed memories without any globally shared memory. For these machines, communication between the processors becomes a bottleneck because accessing memories of remote processors takes more time than accessing the shared memory in the shared memory machine. Thus, minimizing communications between the processors becomes the most important consideration in developing algorithms on distributed memory machines. This makes algorithm development and implementation on distributed memory machines more challenging. The neural dynamics model presented in the previous chapters is highly stable and has excellent convergence properties, especially for optimization of large structures with thousands of members subjected to the actual highly nonlinear and implicit constraints of the design codes. Further, it lends itself to effective parallel processing. In this chapter we present distributed nonlinear neural dynamics algorithms for discrete optimization of large structures. The algorithms are implemented on a distributed memory machine, the CRAY T3D, introduced to the market in 1993, and applied to the minimum weight design of three large steel structures ranging in size from 1,310 to 8,904 members. In the following sections the architecture of the CRAY T3D and the data parallel and work sharing programming models used in this work are described first. Then, distributed algorithms are presented in detail. Finally, three large example steel structures and performance results are presented.

8.2   Cray T3D System Architecture and Programming Model

Introduced to the market in 1993, the main components of the CRAY T3D system (Figure 8.1) are the processing nodes, an interconnection network, and input/output gateways (CRI, 1993a). A processing node has two processing elements (PE). As the basic computational unit, each PE consists of a microprocessor with a peak performance of 150 million floating point operations per second (MFLOPS) and local memory of 8

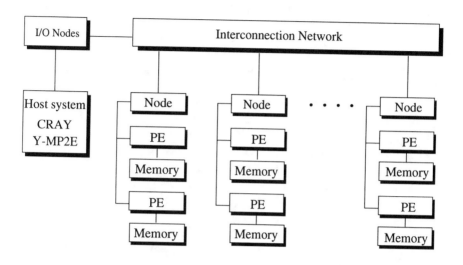

FIGURE 8.1 Main components of CRAY T3D system

Mwords (64MB). A CRAY T3D may consist of $2^5 = 32$ to 2^{11} = 2,048 PEs and is classified as a massively parallel processing (MPP) system. Communication among the processing nodes is through the interconnection network. The performance of distributed processing algorithms is highly dependent on the interconnection topology of the distributed memory system. Processing nodes in the CRAY T3D system are connected in a three-dimensional torus (Figure 8.2) where each processing node has six communication links in both positive and negative X-, Y-, and Z-directions, with a peak communication rate of 300MB/s (CRI, 1993a). A torus network provides a fault tolerant interconnection where the failure of one communication link of a processor does not result in a crash. Another advantage is efficiency of the communication. For example, in Figure 8.2, if processing node A needs to communicate with processing node

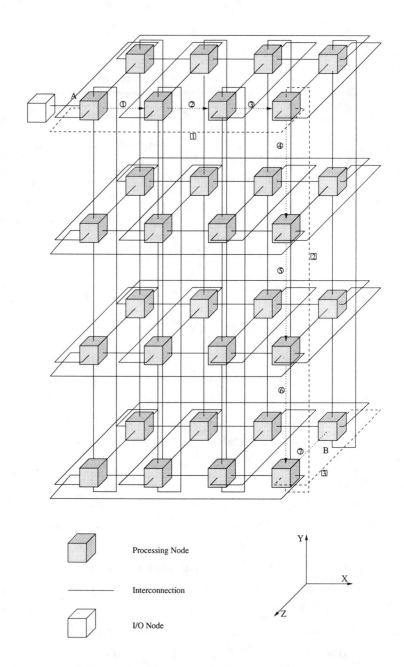

Processing Node

Interconnection

I/O Node

FIGURE 8.2 Cray T3D torus interconnection

B, the communication will be done through the dashed line requiring a maximum of three hops for the 32-node configuration (identified by numbers in squares). Without the torus interconnection, the communication had to be done through the dotted line requiring a maximum of seven hops for the 32-node configuration (identified by number in circles). The CRAY T3D system must be connected to a host computer for compilation. The host system also has its own memory for the storage of data. For the CRAY T3D used in this work, the host is a CRAY Y-MP 2E supercomputer with 32Mwords of memory. All input/output communications between the CRAY T3D and the host systems is performed through the input/output node (Figure 8.2). Applications developed for the CRAY T3D system are compiled on the host system and run on the CRAY T3D. Data objects (scalar or array data) on the CRAY T3D system are divided into private and shared data. Each PE initially receives the same copy of the private data object but can modify it during the program execution. As such, the same private data variable may be assigned different values in different PEs. The shared data, on the other hand, are divided among PEs (each PE receives only a portion of it). Shared scalars are allocated to a single PE (usually PE 0) and shared arrays are distributed among PEs according to the mechanisms specified by the algorithm. Currently, shared arrays are allowed to be distributed by the dimensional distribution such as cyclic, generalized, block, and degenerated distributions (CRI, 1993b). On the CRAY T3D system, a program executes in three different regions: parallel, serial, and work-sharing regions. The program starts to execute in the parallel region where all the PEs execute concurrently on the same section of the code. The serial region is where the section of a code is executed by a single processor explicitly specified by the algorithm. In the work-sharing loops, iterations are distributed across available PEs, and each PE independently executes the iterations allocated to that PE. Mechanisms for allocating iterations to the available PEs must be specified in the algorithm to achieve maximum data locality and load balancing.

8.3   Distributed Algorithms

8.3.1   Recalling available cross-sectional properties

The trained counterpropagation neural network is linked to the neural dynamics model as the database manager. The counterpropagation network is trained using a set of W shapes available in the AISC ASD and LRFD manuals (AISC, 1989 & 1994). At every design iteration, the improved values of design variables obtained from the neural dynamics model are concurrently mapped to commercially available W shapes and their corresponding cross-sectional properties. The recalling process in the counterpropagation network is done in two steps. In the first step, a competition is created among the nodes in the competition layer (whose connection weights are the set of available cross-sectional areas) for each design variable to select the winning node (whose connection weight is closest to the input but not smaller). In the second step, the connection weights (available cross-sectional properties) associated with the winning node are recalled.

In the first step, the competition is defined by the selection of minimum distance between the ith design variable, X_i ($i = 1$, K), and the connection weights U_{ij} between this variable and the T available standard shapes

$$
d_{ij} = \begin{cases} \parallel U_{ij} - X_i \parallel if & U_{ij} \geq X_i \\ & \qquad i = 1,\ K \quad and \quad j = 1,\ T \ (8.1) \\ 0 & if \quad U_{ij} < X_i \end{cases}
$$

The number of competitions involved at any given iteration is the same as the number of design variables (K). This step is done concurrently by assigning each competition to a PE. If the number of PEs available is N_p, then the number of competitions executed on each PE is K/N_p (rounded up to the nearest integer). Each competition requires communications among PEs where $\mathbf{U}$ is stored and the PEs where $\mathbf{X}$ is allocated. This communication, requiring access to remote PEs, can be avoided only if X_i, and U_{ij} are allocated to the same PE. By broadcasting multiple copies (private arrays) of $\mathbf{U}$ to the available PEs, each PE has K/N_p number of design variables and its own copy of $\mathbf{U}$. Thus, a PE performs K/N_p competitions concurrently without communications. The selection of the winning node for each design variable is also done without communications because each PE computes the Euclidean distances and selects the minimum of those distances using local data of the design variable and the connection weights assigned to the PE.

After selection of the winning nodes for the design variables, the recalling process for the required cross-sectional properties is done locally by broadcasting private copies of cross-sectional properties to the available PEs. Thus, the computation involved in the recalling process is shared and executed concurrently on the available PEs.

8.3.2 Work-sharing preconditioned conjugate gradient algorithm

For the solution of the resulting linear simultaneous equations, a distributed preconditioned conjugate gradient (PCG) algorithm is developed employing the work sharing programming paradigm. Parallelism is exploited at both node and member levels by allocating each member of the structure and nodal degree of freedom to a PE. The cross-sectional properties needed for generation of element stiffness matrices are obtained from the trained CPN and distributed among PEs. Each PE generates $N_m = M/N_p$ element stiffness matrices (rounded up to the next integer). Computations involved in the element stiffness matrix generations are shared over the available PEs without assembling a global stiffness matrix. In order to accelerate the search process, a diagonal preconditioner is used by assembling the diagonal components of the element stiffness matrices (Golub and Loan, 1989). The preconditioner is a vector whose number of elements is equal to the number of degrees of freedom of the structure (N_d).

$N_{dp} = N_d/N_p$ (rounded up to the nearest integer) is roughly the number of degrees of freedom assigned to each processor. Also, all the vectors required in the PCG algorithm such as nodal loads, nodal displacements, and residual and search direction vectors are distributed across the available processors. Consequently, vector update operations among the nodewise vectors previously mentioned are performed across the processors with no communications. Dot products between two vectors distributed over the processors, however, require communications due to the global summation of all elements, followed by the multiplication of the two vectors. To minimize the communication cost, the dot product is performed in three steps (Figure

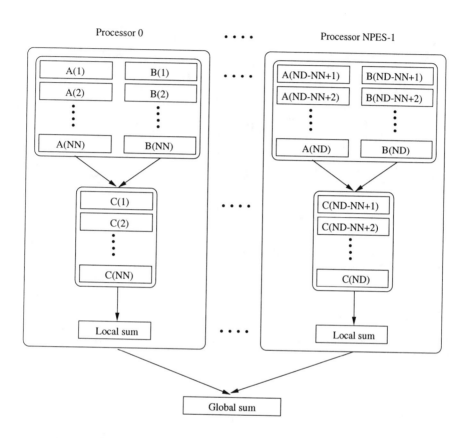

FIGURE 8.3 Distributed dot product operation

8.3). In step one, N_{dp} elements of vectors allocated to the same processor are multiplied and stored in its local memory. In step two, each processor performs local summations on the resulting elements from the multiplication stored only in its own memory. In the third and final step, global summation is calculated using the local sums located on the processors. Hence, the communication is only required one time for the global summation. In computations of the search direction and residual vectors at any

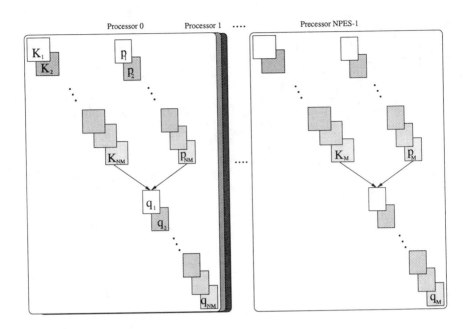

FIGURE 8.4 Distributed matrix/vector multiplication

PCG iteration, the major computation is the matrix vector multiplication between the stiffness matrix ($\mathbf{K}$) and the search direction vector ($\mathbf{p}$). The nodewise direction vector is transformed to the element level direction matrix for element level matrix-matrix multiplication with no communications. The N_m number of element stiffness and direction matrices are assigned to each processor (Figure 8.4). The dimensions of element stiffness and direction matrices are $2N_2 X 2N_2 X M$ and $2N_2 X M$, respectively. N_2 is the number of nodal degrees of freedom per node ($N_2 = 3$ and 6 for truss and frame elements, respectively). Therefore, each processor executes matrix-matrix multiplications and summations concurrently using the local data residing on its own local memory. The resulting memberwise direction matrix

$\mathbf{q}(2N_2XM)$ is transformed to the nodewise direction vector and used for the remaining node level computations in the PCG algorithm.

The PCG algorithm parallelized at element and nodal degree of freedom levels is summarized in the following steps;

step 1. Set up the diagonal preconditioner ($\mathbf{D}$) using the nodal displacement connectivity matrix **IDJ** ($2N_2$, M) and lay out its elements across the local memories of PEs by a degree of freedom per PE. (In steps 2 and 3, N_d iterations are distributed across the PEs. Thus, each PE executes roughly N_d/N_p, rounded up to the nearest integer, iterations concurrently.)

step 2. Calculate the initial residual (error) vector ($\mathbf{r}_0$) and use it as initial search director vector ($\mathbf{p}_0$), and compute the temporary vector $\mathbf{z}_0$ and the initial value of the scalar, ρ_0, concurrently at the degree-of-freedom level using a starting nodal displacement vector ($\mathbf{u}_0$) $=0$.

$$\mathbf{r}_0(1:N_d) = \mathbf{P}(1:N_d)$$
$$-\mathbf{K}(2N_2, 2N_2, M)\mathbf{u}_0(1:N_d) \qquad (8.2)$$
$$\mathbf{p}_0(1:N_d) = \mathbf{r}_0(1:N_d), \qquad (8.3)$$
$$\mathbf{z}_0(1:N_d) = \mathbf{D}^{-1}(1:N_d)\mathbf{r}_0(1:N_d), \quad and \qquad (8.4)$$
$$\rho_0 = \mathbf{z}_0^T(1:N_d) \cdot \mathbf{r}_0(1:N_d) \qquad (8.5)$$

step 3. Check the convergence of the PCG algorithm using the norm of the residual (error) vector, $\mathbf{r}$. If $\| \mathbf{r} \| \leq \varepsilon$, then $\mathbf{u}$ is the nodal displacement vector, and stop. Otherwise do the following steps: (In steps 4-6, M iterations are distributed across the PEs. Thus, each PE excecutes roughly M/N_p, rounded up to the nearest integer, iterations concurrently.)

step 4. Transform the direction vector into a temporary two-dimensional matrix using the nodal displacement connectivity matrix $\mathbf{IDJ}(2N_2, M)$.
ptemp $(2N_2, M) = \mathbf{p}\,[\mathbf{IDJ}\,(2N_2, M)]$

step 5. Do the concurrent matrix-matrix multiplications at the element level.
$\mathbf{vtemp}(2N_2, M) = \mathbf{K}(2N_2, 2N_2, M)\mathbf{ptemp}(2N_2, M)$

step 6. Transform the matrix **ptemp** into the vector $\mathbf{v}(Nd)$ using the connectivity matrix $\mathbf{IDJ}(2N_2, M)$.
$\mathbf{v}[\mathbf{IDJ}(2N_2, M)] = \mathbf{v}[\mathbf{IDJ}(2N_2, M)] + \mathbf{ptemp}(2N_2, M)$

(In the following steps, N_d iterations are distributed across PEs. Thus, each PE executes roughly N_d/N_p iterations concurrently)

step 7. Compute the step size for the search direction, $\gamma = \rho/\alpha$, where
$\alpha = \mathbf{p}^T(N_d) \cdot \mathbf{v}(N_d)$

step 8. Compute the improved nodal displacement vector.
$\mathbf{u}(1 : N_d) = \mathbf{u}(1 : N_d) + \gamma\mathbf{p}(1 : N_d)$

step 9. Calculate the new residual vector.
$\mathbf{r}(1 : N_d) = \mathbf{r}(1 : N_d) + \gamma\mathbf{p}(1 : N_d)$

step 10. Compute the new search direction vector.
$\mathbf{p}(1 : N_d) = \mathbf{z}(1 : N_d) + \beta\mathbf{p}(1 : N_d)$
$\mathbf{z}(1 : N_d) = \mathbf{M}^{-1}(1 : N_d)\mathbf{r}(1 : N_d)$
$\rho_i = \mathbf{z}(N_d)_0^T \cdot \mathbf{r}(N_d)]$
$\beta = \rho_i/\rho_{i-1}$
Go to Step 3

8.3.3 Constraint evaluation

Displacement constraints can be directly evaluated using the nodal displacement vector from the PCG solver. For stress constraints, the AISD ASD (AISC, 1989) or LRFD (AISC, 1994) specifications are considered. Constraints' evaluations, according to the code specifications, require cross-sectional properties of W shapes for members of the structure. These are provided from the trained CPN. The cross-sectional properties from the CPN network are distributed memberwise such that all sectional properties of a member reside in the memory of a single PE. The N_m number of allowable member stresses or nominal member strengths are computed on each single processor. Thus, the computations related to constraints' evaluations are parallelized at the member level.

8.3.4 Dynamical system

In a neural network model, the input to a node is calculated by the weighted sum of output from the nodes in the previous layer. In our model, the input to the ith node in the variable layer is the sum of three terms (see Eq. 7.7): the inhibitory recurrent connection weight of the *ith* node in the variable layer, C_i; the weighted sum of outputs from the nodes representing member stress constraints in the constraint layer, $\sum_{j=1}^{M} O_{cj} w_{ji}$; and the weighted sum of outputs in the constraint layer, $\sum_{k=1}^{N} O_{ck} w_{ki}$. In the dynamic system, the computations of the inputs of nodes in the variable layer (see Eq. 7.7) are parallelized at both node and connection weight levels. For node level parallelism, the computations of outputs of the nodes in the constraint and variable layers are shared by PEs by distributing nodes in the constraint and variable layers across the

PEs. Thus, each PE computes roughly $N_3 = M + N/N_p$ and $N_1 = K/N_p$ (rounded up to the nearest integer) outputs of the nodes in the constraint and variable layers, respectively. To distribute the computations of inputs to the nodes in the variable layer, each column of the matrix w_{ji} representing connection weights among the ith node in the variable layer and the nodes $(j = 1, M + N)$ in the constraint layer, is assigned to a PE. For the computation of the input to the ith node in the variable layer, $M + N - 1$ remote accesses are required because the ith column of the matrix $\mathbf{w}$ must be multiplied by the vectors of outputs from the nodes in the constraints layer. To minimize this communication requirement, multiple copies of O_{cj} and O_{ck} are broadcasted to all PEs after computations of outputs from the nodes in the constraint layer on the distributed PEs. The values of the improved variables (outputs from the nodes in the variable layer) are computed concurrently on distributed PEs as follows;

step 1. Broadcast multiple copies of O_{cj} and O_{ck} to the PEs by declaring them as a private vector. (In the following steps, K iterations are distributed across the PEs. Consequently, each PE executes roughly N_1 iterations concurrently.)

step 2. Calculate the weighted sum of outputs from the nodes in the constraint layer (concurrent processing at node and weight levels).

$$\dot{\mathbf{X}}(1:K) = -\sum_{j=1}^{M} \mathbf{O}_c(j)\mathbf{w}(j, 1:K)$$
$$-\sum_{k=1}^{N} \mathbf{O}_c(k)\mathbf{w}(k, 1:K) \qquad (8.6)$$

step 3. Calculate the inputs to the nodes in the variable layer (concurrent processing at the node level).

$$\dot{\mathbf{X}}(1:K) = \dot{\mathbf{X}}(1:K) - \mathbf{C}(1:K) \qquad (8.7)$$

step 4. Calculate the outputs of the nodes in the variable layer (improved values of the design variables) by numerical integration (concurrent processing at the node level).

$$\mathbf{X}(1:K) = \mathbf{X}(1:K) + \int \dot{\mathbf{X}}(1:K) \qquad (8.8)$$

8.4   Examples

The distributed structural optimization algorithm is implemented on the CRAY T3D system using the MPP Fortran (CRI, 1993c). To achieve efficient load balancing and maximum data locality, shared arrays are distributed by cyclic distribution. The algorithms are applied to minimum weight design of three large steel structures. Examples 1 and 3 are space axial-load (truss) structures. Example 2 is a space moment-resisting frame with cross bracings. The modulus of elasticity is E=198.91 GPa(29,000 ksi) and the specific weight is ρ=79.97 kN/m^3 (490.0 lb/ft^3). The yield stress of F_y=344.75 MPa(50ksi) is used for all the examples.

8.4.1   Example 1

This example is a 1,310-bar space truss structure modeling the exterior envelope of a 37-story steel high-rise building structure (Figure 5.9). The structure has 332 nodes and is doubly symmetric in the plan. It has an aspect ratio of 7.2. The 1,310 members of the structure are divided into 105 groups. In the three main sections of the structure the same standard W shape is used for vertical members in every two stories, and the same W shape is used for horizontal members with the same length in each floor (there is only one type of horizontal members in sections 1 and 3 and two different types of horizontal members in section 2). The same W shape is used for inclined members in every story. In the two tapered transitional zones where the plan of the structure is reduced, we have only inclined members that are grouped into one group in each tapered zone. For displacement constraints, the interstory drift is limited to 0.004 times the story height in x- and y-directions. The equivalent of a uniform vertical load of 1.92 kPa (40.0 psf) is assigned to the nodes of each floor. The lateral loads due to wind are computed according to the Uniform Building Code(UBC, 1994). Lateral forces are determined by assuming a basic wind speed of 113 km/h (70 mi/h), exposure C (generally open area), and an importance factor of 1. The lower and upper bounds for the selected set of 61 W shapes are 24.71 (3.83) and 1,387.09 cm^2 (215.00 in^2). The required cross-sectional properties for both ASD and LRFD specifications are the cross-sectional area (A) and the radius of gyration (r_y). Therefore, the number of nodes in the competition and interpolation layers are 61 and 2, respectively. For design based on the AISC ASD code, a minimum weight of 4.13 MN (928.64 kips) is found after 15 iterations. This translates into 0.68 kPa (14.84 psf) when the total weight of the structure is divided by the total floor area provided by the structure.

8.4.2 Example 2

Example 2 is a 36-story irregular steel moment-resisting space frame with setbacks and cross bracings (Figures 7.4 and 7.5). The properties, loadings, and lower-bound and upper-bound values for this example are the same as those presented in Section 7.5.1. Based on the relationship between the cross-sectional area and other cross-sectional properties (moments of inertia for beams and radii of gyration for columns and bracings), 162 W shapes were selected as economical beams and 61 W shapes were chosen as economical columns. As such, the number of nodes in the competition and interpolation layers are 223 (162 + 61) and 3, respectively.

Minimum weights of 21.51 MN (4,836.6 kips) and 20.34 MN (4,573.5 kips) are obtained using the ASD and LRFD codes, respectively. These numbers translate into 0.59 (12.44) and 0.56 kPa (11.76 psf) for ASD and LRFD codes, respectively, when the total weight of the structure is divided by the total floor area provided by the structure. The minimum weight design based on the LRFD code is 5.4% lighter than that based on the ASD code.

8.4.3 Example 3

Example 3 is a large steel space structure modeling the exterior envelope of a 147-story superhigh-rise steel building structure (Figure 6.6). The properties and vertical loads, and lower- and upper-bound values are the same as those given in Section 6.4.3. The lateral loads due to wind are computed according to the Normal Force Method in Uniform Building Code (UBC) (1994). Lateral forces are determined by assuming a basic wind speed of 113 km/h (70 mph), exposure C (generally open area),

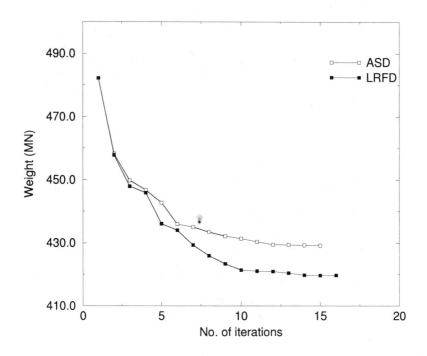

FIGURE 8.5 Convergence histories for Example 3

and an importance factor of 1.

The required cross-sectional properties for this example are the cross-sectional area and the radius of gyration (r_y). Therefore, the numbers of nodes in the competition and interpolation layers are 75 and 2, respectively.

The convergence histories for designs based on AISC ASD and LRFD codes are shown in Figure 8.5. Minimum weights of 429.5 MN (96,564.3 kips) and 419.7 MN (94,354.8 kips) are obtained using the ASD and LRFD codes, respectively. The minimum weight design based on the LRFD code is 2.3% higher than that based on the ASD code.

8.5 Conclusions and Final Comments

Robust and efficient distributed algorithms were presented for discrete optimization of large structure subjected to the actual constraints of commonly used codes employing a combination of data parallel and work-sharing programming models. The algorithms were implemented on the CRAY T3D system and applied to three large steel structures. Mechanisms for allocation iterations to the available PEs were specified in the algorithms in order to achieve maximum data locality and load balancing.

On distributed memory architecture, the limited local memory of each processor creates an obstacle that must be overcome through algorithmic structuring. A distributed preconditioned conjugate gradient algorithm was developed employing the work-sharing programming paradigm and by exploiting parallelism at both node and member levels. The parallel processing speedup curves in Figure 8.6 clearly show the efficiency of the distributed algorithms for optimization of large structures consisting of thousands of members. Speedup is defined as the ratio of execution time on one processing node (two PEs) to execution time on n processing nodes (2n PEs). The efficiency is defined as the speedup divided by the number of processors. For the largest example, a high parallel processing efficiency of 94% is achieved using a 32-processor configuration.

We created and ran two more examples in order to test and

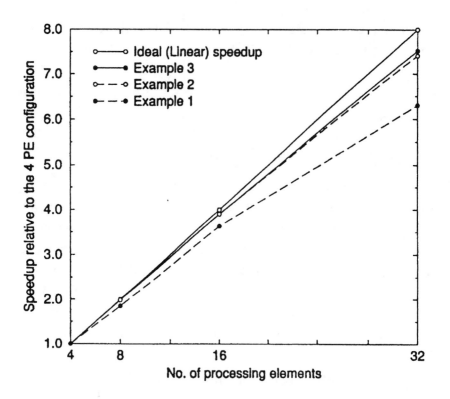

FIGURE 8.6 Relative speedup curves for examples

demonstrate the convergence properties and stability of the algorithms developed in this research. The first example is a highly irregular five-story space moment-resisting steel frame structure shown in Figure 8.7. The next example is a circular 144-story superhigh-rise building structure with variable setbacks shown in Figure 8.8. The convergence histories for this structure using both AISC ASD and LRFD codes are shown in Figure 8.9.

In conclusion, the neural dynamics model and the distributed algorithms developed by the authors have excellent convergence properties and are highly stable. It is particularly noteworthy that they work for structures of any complicated configuration and large size that are subjected to the actual highly nonlinear and implicit constraints of commonly used design codes, such as the AISC LRFD code.

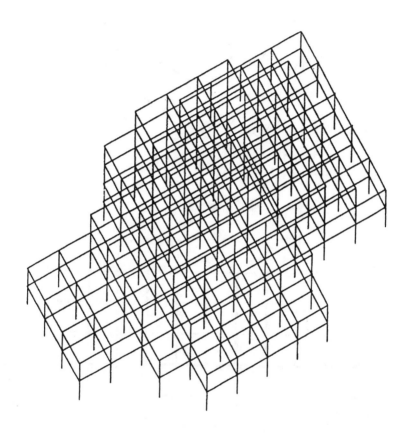

(a) Steel frame

FIGURE 8.7 Irregular five-story moment-resisting steel frame structure

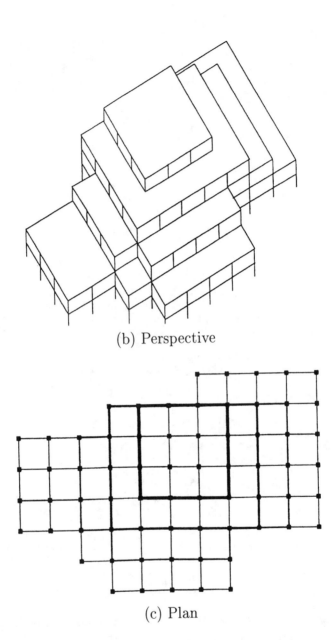

(b) Perspective

(c) Plan

FIGURE 8.7 Irregular five-story moment-resisting steel frame structure - continued

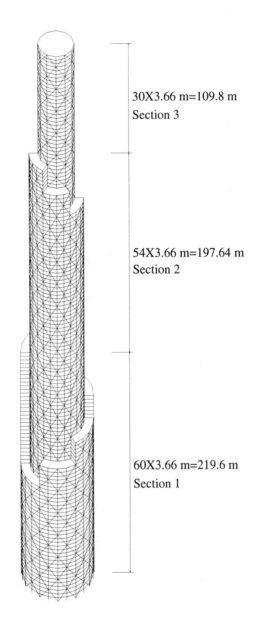

30X3.66 m=109.8 m
Section 3

54X3.66 m=197.64 m
Section 2

60X3.66 m=219.6 m
Section 1

(a) Perspective

FIGURE 8.8 Circular 144-story superhigh-rise building structure with variable setbacks

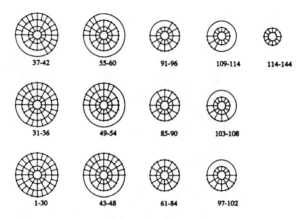

(b) Plans at various heights (Numbers identify stories)

FIGURE 8.8   Circular 144-story superhigh-rise building structure with variable setbacks-continued

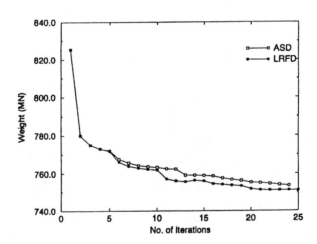

FIGURE 8.9 Convergence histories for structure of figure 8.8

References

Abuyounes, S. and Adeli, H. (1987), "Optimization of Hybrid Steel Plate Girders," *Computers and Structures*, Vol. 27, No. 2, pp. 241-248.

Adeli, H., (1988), *Interactive Microcomputer-Aided Structural Steel Design*, Prentice Hall, Englewood Cliffs, NJ.

Adeli, H., Ed. (1992a), *Supercomputing in Engineering Analysis*, Marcel-Dekker, New York.

Adeli, H., Ed. (1992b), *Parallel Processing in Computational Mechanics*, Marcel Dekker, New York.

Adeli, H., Ed. (1994), *Advances in Design Optimization*, Chapman and Hall, London.

Adeli, H. and Alrijleh, M.M. (1987), "A Knowledge-Based Expert System for Design of Roof Trusses," *Microcomputers in Civil Engineering*, Vol. 2, No. 3, pp. 179-195.

Adeli, H. and Balasubramanyam, K. V. (1988), *Expert Systems for Structural Design*, Prentice Hall, Englewood Cliffs, NJ.

Adeli, H. and Cheng, N.-T. (1993), "Integrated Genetic Algorithm for Optimization of Space Structures," *Journal of Aerospace Engineering*, ASCE, Vol. 6, No. 4, pp. 315-328.

Adeli, H. and Cheng, N.-T. (1994a), "An Augmented Lagrangian Genetic Algorithm for Structural Optimization," *Journal of Aerospace Engineering*, ASCE, Vol. 7, No. 1, pp. 104-118.

Adeli, H. and Cheng, N.-T. (1994b), "Concurrent Genetic Algorithms for Optimization of Large Structures," *Journal of Aerospace Engineering*, ASCE, Vol. 7, No. 3, pp. 276-296.

Adeli, H. and Chompooming, K. (1989), "Interactive Optimization of Nonprismatic Girders," *Computers and Structures*, Vol. 31, No. 4, 1989, pp. 502-522.

Adeli, H. and Chyou, H. H. (1986), "Plastic Analysis of Irregular Frames on Microcomputers," *Computers and Structure*, Vol. 23, No. 2, pp. 233-240

Adeli, H. and Chyou, H. H. (1987), "Microcomputer-Aided Optimum Plastic Design of Frames," *Journal of Computing in Civil Engineering*, ASCE, Vol. 1, No. 1, pp. 20-34

Adeli, H. and Ge. Y. (1989), "A Dynamic Programming Method for Analysis of Bridges Under Multiple Moving Loads," *International Journal for Numerical Methods in Engineering*, Vol. 28, pp. 1265-1282.

Adeli, H. and Hawkins, D. (1991), "A Hierarchical Expert System for Design of Floors in Highrise Buildings," *Computers and Structures*, Vol. 41, No. 4, pp. 773-788.

Adeli, H. and Hung, S. L. (1993a), "A Concurrent Adaptive Conjugate Gradient Learning Algorithm on MIMD Shared-Memory Machines," *Journal of Supercomputer Applications*, Vol. 7, No. 2, pp. 155-156.

Adeli, H. and Hung, S. L. (1993b), "A Fuzzy Neural Network Learning Model for Image Recognition," *Integrated Computer-Aided Engineering*, Vol. 1, No. 1, pp. 43-55.

Adeli, H. and Hung, S.L. (1994), "An Adaptive Conjugate Gradient Learning Algorithm for Effective Training of Multilayer Neural Networks," *Applied Mathematics and Computation*, Vol. 62, No. 1, pp. 81-102.

Adeli, H. and Hung, S. L. (1995), *Machine Learning - Neural Networks, Genetic Algorithms, and Fuzzy Systems*, John Wiley and Sons, New York.

Adeli, H. and Kamal, O. (1986), "Efficient Optimization of Space Trusses," *Computers and Structures*, Vol. 24, No. 3., pp. 501-511.

Adeli, H. and Kamal, O. (1993), *Parallel Processing in Structural Engineering*, Elsevier Science Publishers, London.

Adeli, H., Kamat, M., Kulkarni, G., and Vanluchene, D.(1993), "High Performance Computing Methods in Structural Mechanics and Engineering," *Journal of Aerospace Engineering*, ASCE. Vol. 6, No. 3, pp. 249-267.

Adeli, H. and Kao, W.-M. (1996), "Object-Oriented Blackboard Models for Integrated Design of Steel Structures," *Computers and Structures*, Vol. 61, No. 3, pp. 545-561.

Adeli, H. and Kumar, S. (1995a), "Distributed Genetic Algorithm for Structural Optimization," *Journal of Aerospace Engineering*, Vol. 8, No. 3, pp. 156-163.

Adeli, H. and Kumar, S. (1995b), "Distributed Finite Element Analysis on a Network of Workstations - Algorithms," *Journal of Structural Engineering*, ASCE, Vol. 121, No. 10, pp. 1448-1455.

Adeli, H. and Kumar, S. (1995c), "Concurrent Structural Optimization on a Massively Parallel Supercomputer," *Journal of Structural Engineering*, ASCE, Vol. 121, No. 11, pp. 1588 - 1597.

Adeli, H. and Mabrouk, N. S. (1986), "Optimum Plastic Design of Unbraced Frames of Irregular Configuration," *International Journal of Solids and Structures*, Vol. 22, No. 10, pp. 1117-1128.

Adeli, H. and Mark, K. (1988), "Architecture of a Coupled Expert System for Optimum Design of Plate Girder Bridges," *Engineering Applications of Artificial Intelligence*, Vol. 1, No. 4, pp. 277-285.

Adeli, H. and Mark, K. (1990), "Interactive Optimization of Plate Girder Bridges Subjected to Moving Loads," *Computer-Aided Design*, Vol. 22, No. 6, pp. 368-376.

Adeli, H. and Park, H. S. (1995a), "A Neural Dynamics Model for Structural Optimization - Theory," *Computers and Struc-*

tures, Vol. 57, No. 3, pp. 391-399.

Adeli, H. and Park, H. S. (1995b), "Counter Propagation Neural Networks in Structural Engineering," *Journal of Structural Engineering*, ASCE, Vol. 121, No. 8, pp. 1205-1212.

Adeli, H. and Park, H. S. (1995c), "Optimization of Space Structures by Neural Dynamics Model," *Neural Networks*, Vol. 8, No. 5, pp. 769-781.

Adeli, H. and Park, H. S. (1996a), "Hybrid CPN-Neural Dynamics Model for Discrete Optimization of Steel Structures," *Microcomputers in Civil Engineering*, Vol. 11, No. 5, pp. 355-366.

Adeli, H. and Park, H. S. (1996b), "Fully Automated Design of Super-High-Rise Structures by a Hybrid AI Model on a Massively Parallel Machines," *AI Magazine*, Vol. 17, No. 3, pp. 87-93.

Adeli, H. and Saleh, A. (1997), "Optimal Control of Adaptive/Smart Bridge Structures," *Journal of Structural Engineering*, ASCE, Vol. 123, No. 2, pp. 218-226.

Adeli, H. and Saleh, A. (1998), "Integrated Structural/Control Optimization of Large Adaptive/Smart Structures," *International Journal of Solids and Structures*, to be published.

Adeli, H. and Sarma, K.C. (1995), "Effect of General Sparse Matrix Algorithm on the Optimization of Space Structures," *AIAA Journal*, Vol. 33, No. 12, pp. 2442-2444.

Adeli, H. and Yeh, C. (1989), "Perceptron Learning in Engineering Design," *Microcomputers in Civil Engineering*, Vol. 4, No. 4, pp. 247-256.

Adeli, H. and Yeh, C. (1990), "Explanation-Based Machine Learning in Engineering Design," *Engineering Applications of Artificial Intelligence*, Vol. 3, No. 2, pp. 127-137.

Adeli, H. and Yu, G. (1993a), "An Object-Oriented Data Management Model for Numerical Analysis in Engineering," *Microcomputers in Civil Engineering*, Vol. 8, No. 3, pp. 199-209.

Adeli, H. and Yu, G. (1993b), "A Concurrent OOP Model for Computer-Aided Engineering using Blackboard Architecture," *Journal of Parallel Algorithms and Applications*, Vol. 1, No. 4, pp. 315-337.

Adeli, H. and Zhang, J. (1993), "An Improved Perceptron Learning Algorithm," *Neural, Parallel, and Scientific Computations*, Vol. 1, No. 2, pp. 141-152.

AISC (1989), *Manual of Steel Construction, Allowable Stress Design*, American Institute of Steel Construction, Chicago, IL.

AISC (1994), *Manual of Steel Construction, Load and Resistance Factor Design*, American Institute of Steel Construction, Chicago, IL.

Arora, J. S. (1989), *Introduction to Optimum Design*, McGraw-Hill, New York, NY.

Arora, S. J. and Haug, E. J. (1979), "Methods of Design Sensitivity Analysis in Structural Optimization," *AIAA Journal*, Vol. 17, No. 9, pp. 970-974.

Azema-Barac, M. E. (1992), "A Conceptual Framework for Implementing Neural Networks on Massively Parallel Machines," *Proceedings of the Sixth International Parallel Processing Symposium*, IEEE Computer Society Press, Beverly Hills, CA, pp. 527-530.

Chajes, A. (1974), *Principles of Structural Stability Theory*, Prentice Hall, Englewood Cliffs, NJ.

Chen, W. F. and Lui, E. M. (1987), *Structural Stability*, Elsevier, New York, NY.

Chetayev, N. G. (1961), *The Stability of Motion*, Pergamon Press, New York, NY.

Cohen, M. A. and Grossberg, S. (1983), "Absolute Stability of Global Pattern Formation and Parallel Memory Storage by Competitive Neural Networks," *IEEE Transactions on Systems, Man, and Cybernetics*, Vol. 13, No. 5, pp. 815-826.

Cohn, M. Z., Ghost, S. K., and Parimi, S. R. (1972), "Unified Approach to Theory of Plastic Structures," *Journal of the Engineering Mechanics Division*, ASCE, Vol. 98, No. EM5, pp. 1133-1158.

Cohn, M. Z. and Dinovitzer, A. S. (1994), "Application of Structural Optimization," *Journal of Structural Engineering*, ASCE, Vol. 120, No. 2, pp. 617-650.

CRI, (1993a), *CRAY T3D System Architecture Overview Manual*, Cray Research, Inc., Eagen, MN.

CRI, (1993b), *MPP Fortran Programming Model*, Cray Research, Inc., Eagen, MN.

CRI, (1993c), *Programming the CRAY T3D with Fortran*, Cray Research, Inc., Eagen, MN.

Dumonteil, P. (1992), "Simple Equations for Effective Length Factors," *Engineering Journal*, AISC, Third Quarter, pp. 111-115.

Eisenloffel, K. and Adeli, H. (1990), "Imaging Technique for Cable Network Structures," *International Journal of Imaging Systems and Technology*, Vol. 2, No. 3, pp. 157-168.

Eisenloffel, K. and Adeli, H. (1993), "Microcomputer-Aided Design of Tensile Roof Structures," *Computers and Structures*, Vol. 46, No. 1, pp. 157-174.

Golub, G. H. and Loan, C. V. (1989), *Matrix Computations*, 2nd Ed., The Johns Hopkins University Press, Baltimore, MD.

Elkordy, M. F., Chang, K. C., and Lee, G. C. (1994), "A Structural Damage Neural Network Monitoring System," *Microcomputers in Civil Engineering*, Vol. 9, No. 2, pp. 83-96

Ghaboussi, J., Garrett, J. H., and Wu, X. (1991), "Knowledge-Based Modeling of Material Behavior and Neural Networks," *Journal of Engineering Mechanics*, Vol. 117, No. 1, pp. 132-153.

Golub, G. H. and Loan, C. V. (1989), *Matrix Computations*, 2nd Ed., The Johns Hopkins University Press, Baltimore, MD.

Grossberg, S. (1982), *Studies of Mind and Brain*, Reidel Press, Boston.

Gunaratnam, D.J. and Gero, J.S. (1994), "Effect of Representation on the Performance of Neural Networks in Structural Engineering Applications," *Microcomputers in Civil Engineering*, Vol. 9, No. 2, pp. 145-159.

Gupta, A., Kumar, V., and Sameh, A. (1992), "Performance and Scalability of Preconditioned Conjugate Gradient Methods on Parallel Computers," Technical Report TR 92-64, Dept. of Computer Science, U. of Minnesota, Minneapolis, MN.

Hajela, P. and Berke, L. (1991), "Neurobiological Computational Models in Structural Analysis and Design," *Computers and Structures*, Vol. 41, No. 4, pp. 657-667.

Hecht-Nielsen, R. (1987a), "Counterpropagation Networks," *Proceedings of the IEEE First International Conference on Neural Networks*, June 21-24, Vol. II, IEEE Press, San Diego, CA, pp. 19-32.

Hecht-Neilsen, R. (1987b), "Counter Propagation Networks," *Applied Optics*, Vol. 26, No. 23, pp. 4979-4985.

Hecht-Neilsen, R. (1988), "Applications of Counterpropagation Networks," *Neural Networks*, Vol. 1, No. 2, pp. 131-139.

Hegazy, T., Fazio, P., and Moselhi, O. (1994), "Developing Practical Neural Network Applications using Backpropagation," *Microcomputers in Civil Engineering*, Vol. 9, No. 2, pp. 145-159.

Hertz, T., Krogh, A., and Palmer, R. G. (1991), *Introduction to the Theory of Neural Computation*, Addison-Wesley Publishing Company, Redwood City, CA.

Hirsch, M. W. and Smale, S. (1974), *Differential Equations, Dynamical Systems, and Linear Algebra*, Academic Press, New York, NY.

Hopfield, J. (1982), "Neural Networks and Physical Systems with Emergent Collective Computational Abilities," *Proceedings of the National Academy of Sciences*, Vol. 79, No. 8, pp. 2554-2558.

Hopfield, J. (1984), "Neurons with Graded Response Have Collective Computational Properties Like Those of Two-State Neurons," *Proceedings of the National Academy of Sciences*, Vol. 81, No. 10, pp. 3088-3092.

Hopfield, J. J. and Tank, D. W. (1986), " Simple 'Neural' Optimization Networks: An A/D Converter, Signal Decision Circuit, and a Linear Programming Circuit," *IEEE Transactions on Circuits and Systems*, Vol. 33, No. 5, pp. 533-541.

Hua, H. M. (1983), "Optimization for Structures of Discrete-Size Elements," *Computers and Structures*, Vol. 17, No. 3, pp. 327-333.

Hui, S. and Zàk, S. H. (1992), "Dynamical Analysis of the Brain-State-in-a-Box (BSB) Neural Models," *Transactions on Neural*

Networks, Vol. 3, No. 1, pp. 86-94.

Hung, S. L. and Adeli, H. (1991a), "A Model of Perceptron Learning with a Hidden Layer for Engineering Design," *Neurocomputing*, Vol. 3, No. 1, pp. 3-14.

Hung, S. L. and Adeli, H. (1991b), "A Hybrid Learning Algorithm for Distributed Memory Multicomputers," *Heuristics*, Vol. 4, No. 4, pp. 58-68.

Hung, S. L. and Adeli, H. (1993), "Parallel Backpropagation Learning Algorithm on Cray YMP8/864 Supercomputer," *Neurocomputing*, Vol. 5, Vol. 5, pp. 287-302.

Hung, S.L. and Adeli, H. (1994a), "Object-Oriented Backpropagation and Its Applications to Structural Design," *Neurocomputing*, Vol. 6, No. 1, pp. 45-55.

Hung, S.L. and Adeli, H. (1994b), "A Parallel Genetic, Neural Network Learning Algorithm for MIMD Shared Memory Machines," *IEEE Transactions on Neural Networks*, Vol. 5, No. 6, pp. 900-909.

Hurson, A. R., Pakzad, S., and Jin, B. (1994), "Automated Knowledge Acquisition in a Neural Network-Based Decision Support System for Incomplete Database Systems," *Microcomputers in Civil Engineering*, Vol. 9, No. 2, pp. 129-143.

Jayadeva, C. and Bhaumik, B. (1992), "Optimization with Neural Networks: A Recipe for Improving Convergence and Solution Quality," *Biological Cybernetics*, Vol. 67, No. 5, pp. 445-449.

Johnsson, S. L. and Mathur, K. K. (1989), "Experience with the Conjugate Gradient Method for Stress Analysis on a Data Parallel Supercomputers," *International Journal for Numerical Methods in Engineering*, Vol. 27, pp. 523-546.

Johnsson, S. L. and Mathur, K. K. (1990), "Data Structures and Algorithms for the Finite Element Method on a Data Parallel Supercomputer," *International Journal for Numerical Methods in Engineering*, Vol. 29, pp. 881-908.

Kang, H.-T. and Yoon, C. J. (1994), "Neural Network Approaches to Aid Simple Truss Design Problems," *Microcomputers in Civil Engineering*, Vol. 9, No. 2.

Kao, W.-M. and Adeli, H. (1997), "Distributed Object-Oriented Blackboard Model for Integrated Design of Steel Structures," *Microcomputers in Civil Engineering*, Vol. 12, No. 2, pp. 141-154.

Kennedy, M. P. and Chua, L. O. (1988), "Neural Networks for Nonlinear Programming," *IEEE Transactions on Circuits and Systems*, Vol. 35, No. 5, pp. 554-562.

Kitipornchai, S., Wang, C.H., and Trahair, N.S. (1986), "Buckling of Monosymmetric I - Beams under Moment Gradient," *Journal of Structural Division*, ASCE, Vol. 112, No. 4, pp. 781-799.

Kohonen, T. (1988), *Self-organization and Associative Memory*, Springer-Verlag, New York.

Kumar, S. and Adeli, H. (1995a), "Distributed Finite Element

Analysis on a Network of Workstations-Implementation and Application," *Journal of Structural Engineering*, ASCE, Vol. 121, No. 10, pp. 1456-1462.

Kumar, S. and Adeli, H. (1995b), "Minimum Weight Design of Large Structures on a Network of Workstations," *Microcomputers in Civil Engineering*, Vol. 10, No. 6, pp. 423-432.

Liebman, J. S., Khachaturian, N., and Chanaratna, V. (1981), "Discrete Structural Optimization," *Journal of Structural Division*, ASCE, Vol. 107, No. ST11, pp. 2177-2197.

Masri, S. F., Chassiakos, A. G., and Caughey, T. K. (1993), "Identification of Nonlinear Dynamics System Using Neural Networks," *Journal of Applied Mechanics*, ASME, Vol. 60, No. 1, pp. 123-133.

Messner, J. I., Sanvido, V. E., and Kumara, S. R. T. (1994), "StructNet: A Neural Network for Structural System Selection," *Microcomputers in Civil Engineering*, Vol. 9, No. 2, pp. 109-118.

Miyamoto, H., Kawato, M., Setoyama, T., and Suzuki, R. (1988), "Feedback-Error-Learning Neural Network for Trajectory Control of a Robotic Manipulator," *Neural Networks*, Vol. 1, No. 3, pp. 251-265.

Nordstrom, T. and Svensson, B. (1992), "Using and Designing Massively Parallel Computers for Artificial Neural Networks," *Journal of Parallel and Distributed Computing*, Vol. 14, pp. 260-285.

Paek, Y. and Adeli, H. (1988a), "Representation of Structural Design Knowledge in a Symbolic Language," *Journal of Computing in Civil Engineering*, ASCE, Vol. 2, No. 4, pp. 346-364.

Paek, Y. and Adeli, H. (1988b), "STEELEX: A Coupled Expert System for Integrated Design of Steel Structures," *Engineering Applications of Artificial Intelligence*, Vol. 1, No. 3, pp. 170-180.

Papadrakakis, M., Ed. (1993), *Solving Large-Scale Problems in Mechanics*, John Wiley & Sons, Chichester, England.

Park, H. S. and Adeli, H. (1995), "A Neural Dynamics Model for Structural Optimization - Application to Plastic Design of Structures," *Computers and Structures*, Vol. 57, No. 3, pp. 391-399.

Park, H. S. and Adeli, H. (1997a), "Data Parallel Neural Dynamics Model for Integrated Design of Large Steel Structures," *Microcomputers in Civil Engineering*, Vol. 12, pp. 311-326.

Park, H. S. and Adeli, H. (1997b), "Distributed Neural Dynamics Algorithms for Optimization of Large Steel Structures," *Journal of Structural Engineering*, ASCE, Vol. 123, No. 7, pp. 880-888.

Ponnusamy, R., Thakur, R., Choudhary, A., Velamakanni, K., Bozkus, Z., and Fox, G. (1993), "Experimental Performance Evaluation of the CM-5," *Journal of Parallel and Distributed Computing*, Vol. 19, pp. 192-202.

Press, W. H., Flannery, B. P., Teukolsky, S. A., and Vetterling, W. T. (1986), *Numerical Recipes*, Cambridge University Press, New York, NY.

Rajeev, S. and Krishnamoorthy, C. S. (1992), "Discrete Optimization of Structures Using Genetic Algorithms," *Journal of Structural Engineering*, ASCE, Vol. 118, No. 5, pp. 1233 - 1250.

Rumelhart, D., Hinton, G., and Williams, R. (1986), "Learning Representations by Backpropagation Errors," in Rumelhart, D. et al., Eds., *Parallel Distributed Processing*, Vol. 1, MIT Press, Cambridge, MA, pp. 318-362.

Saleh, A. and Adeli, H. (1994a), "Microtasking, Macrotasking, and Autotasking for Structural Optimization," *Journal of Aerospace Engineering*, ASCE, Vol. 7, No. 2, pp. 156-174.

Saleh A. and Adeli, H. (1994b), "Parallel Algorithms for Integrated Structural and Control Optimization," *Journal of Aerospace Engineering*, ASCE. Vol. 7, No. 3, pp. 297-314.

Saleh, A. and Adeli, H. (1996), "Parallel Eigenvalue Algorithms for Large-scale Control-optimization Problems," *Journal of Aerospace Engineering, ASCE*, Vol. 9, No. 3, pp. 70-79.

Saleh, A. and Adeli, H. (1997), "Robust Parallel Algorithms for Solution of the Riccati Equation," *Journal of Aerospace Engineering*, ASCE, Vol. 10, No. 3, pp. 126-133.

Sarma, K. and Adeli, H, (1996), "Sparse Matrix Algorithm for Minimum Weight Design of Large Structures," *Engineering Op-*

timization, Vol. 27, No. 1, pp. 65-85.

Simpson, P. K. (1991), *Artificial Neural Systems*, Pergamon Press, New York, NY.

Soegiarso, R. and Adeli, H. (1994), "Impact of Vectorization on Large-Scale Structural Optimization," *Structural Optimization*, Vol. 7, pp. 117-125.

Soegiarso, R. and Adeli, H. (1995), "Parallel-Vector Algorithms for Analysis of Large Structures," *Journal of Aerospace Engineering*, ASCE, Vol. 8, No. 1, pp. 54-67.

Soegiarso, R. and Adeli, H. (1996), "Optimization of Large Steel Structures using Standard Cross Sections," *Engineering Journal*, AISC, Vol. 33, No. 3, pp. 83-94.

Soegiarso, R. and Adeli, H. (1997a), "Optimal Load and Resistance Factor Design of Steel Space Frame Structures," *Journal of Structural Engineering*, ASCE, Vol. 123, No. 2, pp. 184-192.

Soegiarso, R. and Adeli, H. (1997b), "Optimization of Large Space Frame Steel Structures," *Engineering Journal*, AISC, Vol. 34, No. 2, 1997, pp. 54-60.

Stephens, J. E. and Vanluchene, R. D. (1994), "Integrated Assesment of Seismic Damage in Structures," *Microcomputers in Civil Engineering*, Vol. 9, No. 2, pp. 119-128.

Tagliarini, G. A., Christ J. F., and Page, E. W. (1991), "Optimization Using Neural Network," *Transactions on Computers*,

IEEE, Vol. 40, No. 12, pp. 1347-1358.

Taylor, V. E. and Nour-Omid, B., and Messerschmett, D. G. (1992), "The Effect of Communication Overhead on the Speedup of Parallel 3-D Finite Element Applications," *Proceedings of the Sixth International Parallel Processing Symposium*, IEEE Computer Society Press, Beverly Hills, CA, pp. 531-536.

TMC (1994a), *CM-5 CM Fortran Performance Guide*, Version 2.1, Thinking Machines Corporation, Cambridge, MA.

TMC (1994b), *CMSSL for CM Fortran*, Vol. 1, Version 3.2, Thinking Machines Corporation, Cambridge, MA.

TMC (1994c), *CM Fortran Programming Guide*, Version 2.1, Thinking Machines Corporation, Cambridge, MA.

UBC (1994), *Uniform Building Code, Vol. 2 - Structural Engineering Design Provisions*, International Conference of Building Officials, Whittier, CA.

Vanderplaats, G. N. (1984), *Numerical Optimization Techniques for Engineering Design*, McGraw-Hill, New York, NY.

Van der Vorst, H. A. and Dekker, K. (1988), "Conjugate Gradient Type Methods and Preconditioning," *Journal of Computational and Applied Mathematics*, Vol. 24, pp. 73-87.

Vanluchene, D. and Sun, R. (1990), "Neural Networks in Structural Engineering," *Microcomputers in Civil Engineering*, Vol. 5, No. 3, pp. 207-215.

Venkayya, V. B., Knot, N. S., and Reddy, V. S. (1969), "Energy Distribution in An Optimal Structural Design," AFFDLTR-68-156, Flight Dynamics Laboratory, Wright-Patterson AAFB, Ohio.

Wilson, G. V. and Pawley, G. S. (1988), "On the Stability of the Traveling Salesman Problem Algorithms of Hopfield and Tank," *Biological Cybernetics*, Vol. 58, No. 1, pp. 63-70.

Winget, J. M. and Hughes, T. J. R. (1985), "Solution Algorithms for Nonlinear Transient Heat Conduction Analysis Employing Element-By-Element Iterative Strategies," *Computer Methods In Applied Mechanics And Engineering*, Vol. 52, pp. 711-815.

Woods, D. (1988), "Back and Counter Propagation Aberrations," *Proceedings of the IEEE International Conference on Neural Networks*, Vol. 1, IEEE, pp. 473-479.

Yu, G. and Adeli, H. (1991), "Computer-Aided Design Using Object-Oriented Programming Paradigm and Blackboard Architecture," *Microcomputers in Civil Engineering*, Vol. 6, No. 3, pp. 177-190.

Yu, G. and Adeli, H. (1993), "Object-Oriented Finite Element Analysis Using EER Model," *Journal of Structural Engineering*, ASCE, Vol. 119, No. 9, pp. 2763-2781.

Zhu, D. M. (1986), "An improved Templeman's Algorithm for Optimum Design of Trusses with Discrete Member Sizes," *Engineering Optimization*, Vol. 9, pp. 303-312. 52, pp. 711-815.

Index